VE *dare* YOU

SCRAPBOOK CHALLENGES about real life

kristina contes
meghan heath dymock
genevieve simmonds
nisa fiin

Memory Makers Books
Cincinnati, Ohio

www.memorymakersmagazine.com

We Dare You. Copyright © 2007 by Contes, Dymock, Fiin, Simmonds.
Manufactured in China. All rights reserved. It is permissible for the purchaser to
make the projects contained herein and sell them at fairs, bazaars and craft shows.
No other part of this book may be reproduced in any form or by any electronic or
mechanical means including information storage and retrieval systems without
permission in writing from the publisher, except by a reviewer, who may quote a
brief passage in review. Published by Memory Makers Books, an imprint of F+W
Publications, Inc., 4700 East Galbraith Road, Cincinnati, Ohio 45236. (800) 289-0963.
First edition.

11 10 09 08 07   5 4 3 2 1

Distributed in Canada by Fraser Direct
100 Armstrong Avenue
Georgetown, ON, Canada L7G 5S4
Tel: (905) 877-4411

Distributed in the U.K. and Europe by David & Charles
Brunel House, Newton Abbot, Devon, TQ12 4PU, England
Tel: (+44) 1626 323200, Fax: (+44) 1626 323319
E-mail: postmaster@davidandcharles.co.uk

Distributed in Australia by Capricorn Link
P.O. Box 704, S. Windsor, NSW 2756 Australia
Tel: (02) 4577-3555

Library of Congress Cataloging-in-Publication Data

Contes, Kristina
  We dare you : scrapbook challenges about real life / Kristina Contes ... [et al.].
     p. cm.
  Includes index.
  ISBN-13: 978-1-59963-013-7 (alk. paper)
  1. Photograph albums. 2. Scrapbooks. I. Title.
TR465.C672 2007
745.593--dc22
                          2007015275

Editor: Christine Doyle
Design Concept: Kristina Contes, Meghan Heath Dymock,
                 Genevieve Simmonds, Nisa Fiin
Designer: Jeremy Werling
Art Coordinator: Eileen Aber
Production Coordinator: Matthew Wagner
Photographers: Al Parrish, Kris Kandler, Robert Best
Stylist: Nora Martini

Digital graffiti brushes courtesy
of Jason Gaylor of dragonfruit.com.

www.fwbookstore.com

Post your layouts inspired by these Dares
on our website: www.efferdares.com.

ABOUT THE AUTHORS

Kristi

Nisa

Gen

Meg

Kristina Contes. Loves music, movies, design and fashion. Uses the word "Dude" profusely. Loves her husband Jonathan fiercely. Works at their restaurant, Mosaic. Watches *Law and Order* reruns all day long. Compulsively collects sneakers, also known as "kicks." Went to school for Interior Design, Fine Art and Jewelry Design, with a degree in none. Started the Dares in July of 2005 over IM. Shops, plays and takes pictures in NYC. Dresses her dog Chloe in bomber jackets. Paper crafts like it is her job...which it is now since she has started teaching! Has quite the sarcastic streak about her.

Nisa Fiin lives with her husband Ben and their sweet naked pup Hooper in Minnesota. Nisa is a photographer/artist who loves making a mess, writing upside-down, and buying more paper than a person could ever really need. She is obsessed with books, antique photos and old furniture with drawers. If it has drawers, Nisa must own it. She drinks a jug of cranberry juice a day and is almost always wearing a hoodie. Nisa talks a lot. Even to strangers. If you got points for talking to strangers, Nisa would so be winning. Nisa was in love with the Dares since day one and was thrilled when she was asked to join in 2006. The Dares push her to keep her scrapping real and fresh, and she loves that. Hard.

Genevieve Simmonds is a scrapbooking and mixed media artist, residing in Vancouver, British Columbia, with her husband and son. Art in some form has always had a place in her life, and once she discovered scrapbooking that was it: zero-to-obsessed in 3.5 seconds. The obsession continues into the realm of product design and trying to ignite creative passion in others. When not making a mess with whatever she can get her hands on, she can be found anywhere near her amazing husband, trying to force her son Jaxon to give her cuddles, reading trashy magazines or art books with a glass of fine red wine, or, well, more than likely, sleeping.

Originally from Salt Lake City, Meghan Heath Dymock graduated with her BA in communications from Westminster College in June 2005. A week later she and her sexy, computer-savvy husband moved to Arizona so he could pursue his MBA. Meghan is a founding member of the Dares and loves the honesty, friendships and inspiration they constantly provide. Meghan prefers talking to listening, rainy days to sunny days, has a deep affection for photography, loves being told she is "most fun on the planet" by her mom, huge belly laughs with her sister, mom or best friend, creating art all day, cleaning the house and kissing Tyson.

TABLE OF CONTENTS

accomplishments. Not one to brag, boast or tell everyone I am the shit. Yes, there are things about me I believe to be true. I have awesome Leo hair. I can throw together a funky outfit. I can throw down with some freestyle rhymes. I am fiercely loyal. I have an ever hungry creative spirit. I am ambitious and forward thinking. I am pretty fucking sweet. But often times I focus on the negatives, the setbacks and the what ifs. So today I am reveling in the good. The things that are great. The worthy of ink on my flesh. The positives.

BE PROUD

08.26.2006

her DAY 100%

7

one YOU LOVE GETTING THINGS IN THE MAIL.
two BEFORE YOU GO TO SLEEP, YOU ALWAYS NEED YOUR BACK SCRATCHED.
three TOYS, TOYS, TOYS! THEY'RE ALWAYS ON YOUR MIND.
four YOU THINK THE BEST WAY TO TAKE A BATH IS WITH LOTS AND LOTS OF BUBBLES.
five YOU ONCE SAID, "THE BEST PART ABOUT SCHOOL IS RECESS!"
six EATING IS VERY HARD FOR YOU.
seven YOU LIKE DOING CRAFTS WITH MOMMY AND PLAYING VIDEO GAMES WITH DADDY.

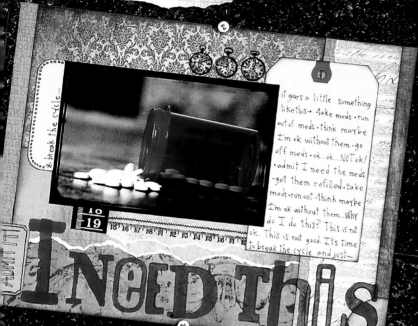

*break the cycle...

ADMIT IT

I NEED THIS

it goes a little something like this: •take meds •run out of meds •think maybe I'm ok without them •go off meds •ok...ok...NOT ok! •admit I need the meds •get them refilled •take meds •run out •think maybe I'm ok without them...Why do I do this? This is not ok. This is not good. It's time to break the cycle and just—

pissed off finds me first. infuriated and mad, screaming and hating everyone before I am hysterical, crying in a heap on the floor. It has been this way always.

"You know that we're going to be friends for like ever right?"

"Well, duh."

who know?

September 2005

that when this picture was taken we'd grow to be such BFF?

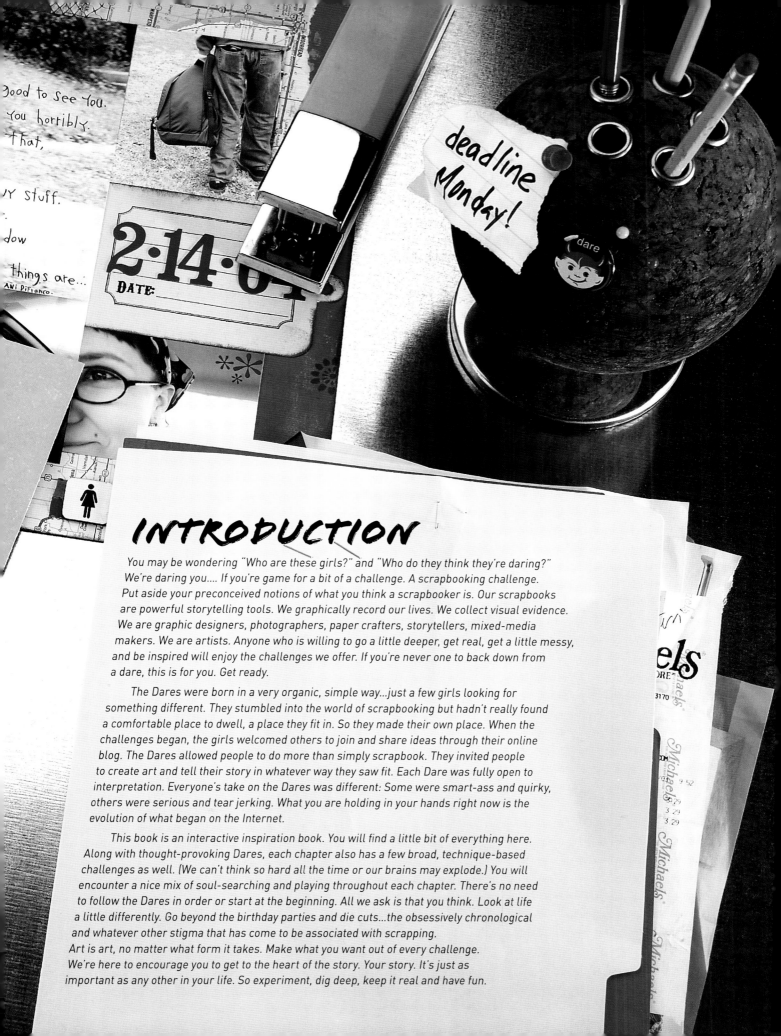

INTRODUCTION

You may be wondering "Who are these girls?" and "Who do they think they're daring?" We're daring you.... If you're game for a bit of a challenge. A scrapbooking challenge. Put aside your preconceived notions of what you think a scrapbooker is. Our scrapbooks are powerful storytelling tools. We graphically record our lives. We collect visual evidence. We are graphic designers, photographers, paper crafters, storytellers, mixed-media makers. We are artists. Anyone who is willing to go a little deeper, get real, get a little messy, and be inspired will enjoy the challenges we offer. If you're never one to back down from a dare, this is for you. Get ready.

The Dares were born in a very organic, simple way...just a few girls looking for something different. They stumbled into the world of scrapbooking but hadn't really found a comfortable place to dwell, a place they fit in. So they made their own place. When the challenges began, the girls welcomed others to join and share ideas through their online blog. The Dares allowed people to do more than simply scrapbook. They invited people to create art and tell their story in whatever way they saw fit. Each Dare was fully open to interpretation. Everyone's take on the Dares was different: Some were smart-ass and quirky, others were serious and tear jerking. What you are holding in your hands right now is the evolution of what began on the Internet.

This book is an interactive inspiration book. You will find a little bit of everything here. Along with thought-provoking Dares, each chapter also has a few broad, technique-based challenges as well. (We can't think so hard all the time or our brains may explode.) You will encounter a nice mix of soul-searching and playing throughout each chapter. There's no need to follow the Dares in order or start at the beginning. All we ask is that you think. Look at life a little differently. Go beyond the birthday parties and die cuts...the obsessively chronological and whatever other stigma that has come to be associated with scrapping.
Art is art, no matter what form it takes. Make what you want out of every challenge. We're here to encourage you to get to the heart of the story. Your story. It's just as important as any other in your life. So experiment, dig deep, keep it real and have fun.

WHINING

trans*ATLANTIC*

I don't come from anywhere. No hometown. No place I come back to. I was born somewhere. I went to school a lot of other places. Now I live somewhere else. For some reason my clearest memory of early childhood is sleeping on the floor of the flight American used to operate from Tampa to London. I remember so many airplanes. There used to be decks of cards. There used to be a dress code. There were seats that faced each other in groups of four. There were air-pockets and ashtrays. I have no accent. No regional colloquialisms. My point of reference, the thing I share with people, seems to be air travel in the 1980s.

THE GOOD

You know. The good things. **Positive, warm and fuzzy things.** The pages you can show to friends and family and reminisce about. Savoring the moment. **Lovely life things.** This chapter is all about **the positive stuff.**

STRENGTH HAS A MILLION FACES

N O dYSFuncTiOnAL LOVE

My childhood was far from normal. But it's all I have & it made me who I am today.

AY CITY

SHOOTING
THE THING
B7599
YOU LOVE

{120
Shadow Lane}

LAUGH
PLAY K
ADORE

1977 another time another

Feels like it anyway. The seventies when the most high-tech gadget in the house was the eight track player and nobody thought to put bike helmets on their kids or less stuff, but sometimes I feel like we had more of what's important. More around. outside. More days spent at the library with mom. More picnics on fall weekends. We didn't have a huge inflatable snow dress-up. More playing make our front yard but we had an advent wreath. We didn't have video games — but we neighborhood-wide games of Star Wars complete with invented actions and dialogue didn't have HDTV but we had nightly dance "concerts" with costumes and a flashlight "spot" turned into wonderful things. but we had crayons and little bits of paper — of paper free to run all over the neighborhood. We didn't feel afraid carefree. At least

POSITIVE SELF TALK:

The good things about yourself or others. The things you are proud of. Like those affirmations people say to themselves in the mirror. Now put them on a scrapbook page and always remember the wonderful things about you. Go ahead, love yourself.

At the time I did this Dare, I felt that a good message for myself was letting the good in and blocking out the bad. I chose to detail the more important positive roles I take on. The background for this page started as a scrap piece of cardstock used to protect my table from paint while working on other projects. The photo was on its way to the scrap heap, too; it had been bent and something spilled on it. I saw these pieces while cleaning up and felt there might be potential there.

Genevieve Simmonds

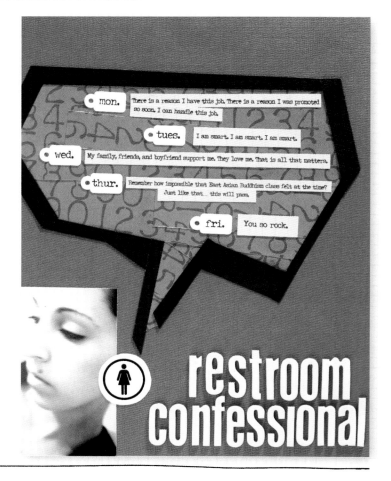

I was drawn to this Dare because I had been having a tough time at work. After a recent promotion, I was stressed out, felt like I was in over my head, and felt like nobody thought I was good enough for my job. I started the habit of going to the bathroom for a "mental break" and reciting positive statements to calm myself down. It really was what got me through the day for a while. By making this page, I am not only honoring myself and my strength during the hard times I had, but I am also revealing a sadness I felt and a struggle I went through.

Jessica Fulkerson

I am generally pretty nonchalant about my accomplishments. Not one to brag, boast or tell everyone why I am the shit. Yes, there are things about me I believe to be true. I have awesome Leo hair. I can throw together a funky outfit. I can throw down with some freestyle rhymes. I am fiercely loyal. I have an ever hungry creative spirit. I am ambitious and forward thinking. I am pretty fucking sweet. But often times I focus on the negatives, the setbacks and the what ifs. So today I am reveling in the good. The things that are great. The worthy of ink on my flesh. The positives.

all about you

BE PROUD

The Dare was to talk yourself up in a positive way. Not something I generally go around doing. So for this Dare I put my normally pessimistic inner critic on hold and focused on my good traits. I used a "You are not here" stamp to convey the idea that I do not normally think of myself in such a positive way. The picture of me in sunglasses also adds to the idea of meekness about being so boastful. Luckily I wasn't too shy and found a few things about myself I actually liked!

Kristina Contes

REPEAT (as needed)

I am brilliant. I am hilarious. I take mad rockin' photos. I sound sooo good when I sing along in the car. I can memorize big numbers and remember them forever. I am amazing with kids. I am easily amused. I can read & write upsidedown. I am creative. I am artsy. I have a knack for picking who will win a reality show from the very first episode. I am here. ☆

REPEAT AS NEEDED

Positive self talk...this is such a good Dare...everyone should do this, so therapeutic. I do a lot of negative thinking, so creating something to remind myself of all the goodness is so good for the soul. I made my own background paper with the phrase "repeat as needed" printed over and over to physically illustrate the idea of "repeat."

Nisa Fiin

SAFE PLACE: Your escape, your refuge, your safe place.

The whole world could be in a state of upheaval, but as long as you can retreat to your place it's all OK. Create a layout that documents wherever, whatever, or whoever makes you feel safe.

For some time now, Dren has been my total safe place. I trust him to do things I had learned to do so that I would never have to rely on anyone to do them for me. I trust him with our child, and I trust him with my friends and loved ones. I trust him with my heart and with my body and soul. I don't know that I have ever felt that before or will ever feel that again with anyone or anything. It's been scary and emotional to let my walls down far enough to feel safe with him. It's still scary, but it's true.

Genevieve Simmonds

I spent quite some time trying to decide where, who or what makes me feel safe. Time and time again I have been told that no one and nothing can center me but myself. God gives me the strength to push through. So I decided to scrap my #1 rule: No matter what, I must go within myself for a sense of calm and security. I chose to use a tiny cluster of photos to convey the feeling of centeredness. I went for a variety of facial expressions to show that whatever my mood may be I can always take a moment, a deep breath and say to myself "I am my safe place."

Kristina Contes

My husband and our relationship is my safe place. Tyson is my strength. He is such a support to me, and when this Dare was brought up, I instantly thought of him and our marriage. This year we faced difficulties we hadn't experienced before, and he was still able to comfort me and be strong for me and for us. The journaling on my arm says: "And she realized she couldn't do it without him 'you'll never have to, he said' we're stronger together with the sparkly stars dancing on our shoulders."

Meghan Heath Dymock

For us, no doubt, the place we go to escape is up North: water, trees, lake. Nothing better. I wanted this one page to look like a whole scrapbook—I wanted it to capture all the awesomeness of our getaways up North. I used lots of little photos, some with individual captions, in addition to the journaling for the page as a whole. I used papers that were primarily blue and green to pick up the colors of the land and water in the photos, with a golden orange as a complementary accent.

Nisa Fiin

OBSESSED:

We all have obsessions. You know you do. Things you can't pass up, things you can't live without. Maybe it's lip gloss, maybe it's a store, or even the rituals that make up your daily life. Scrap 'em. You'll thank us later. Even if it's only to laugh at that crazy fad you thought you couldn't live without.

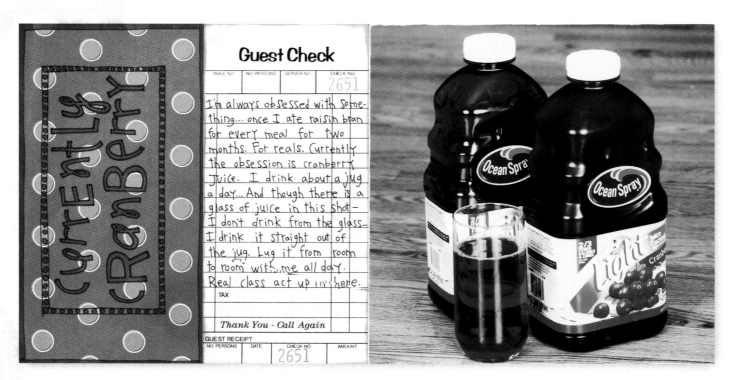

I will admit it: I am an obsessive person. It's always something with me...and currently it's cranberry juice. Delicious. This layout is 6" x 12" (15cm x 30cm). I divided it up into three distinct areas: title, journaling and photo blocks. I wanted it to be very simple and striking. I chose the paper to echo the color and shape of cranberries. I used the "guest check" Photoshop brush because it calls to mind food and drink.

Nisa Fiin

I had just received some brand new sheets of unmounted rubber stamps and wanted to photograph them because they don't stay like that for long. With this page, I wanted to really go nuts expressing my obsession with them. I used one of the journaling line blocks repeatedly, stacking the images vertically to create one long stamped image. I used it as a background for the title and as my journaling space.

Genevieve Simmonds

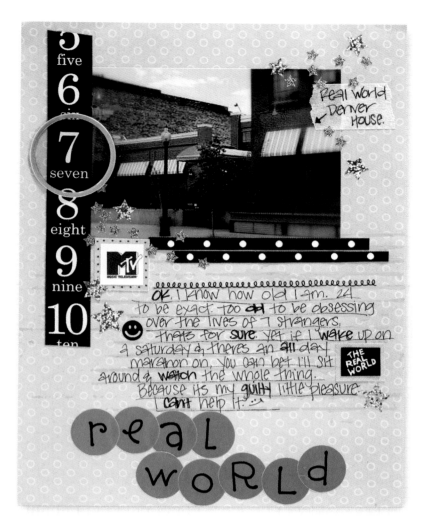

I journaled truthfully about my obsession with *The Real World*, almost to the point of embarrassment. To make the journaling, I painted a piece of cardstock and stamped it. I then lightly ran over it with a pen.

Jamie Bagley

Since one thing I can't stray from for too long is a good city trip, I decided to scrap about all the city dates I go on with my husband. Once I decided on city dates as my theme, I collected all the pictures from over the years and made them the focal point of the layout. I used a subway map to reinforce the theme and journaled about all the hotels and restaurants we've visited. So happy to have a collective place to remember all our city adventures!

Kristina Contes

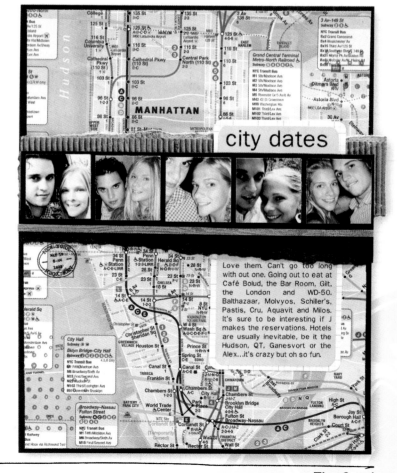

FAVORITE THINGS: *The things or people you hold most dear.*

Your favorite movie. Your favorite jeans. Your favorite photos.
Your favorite uncle. Scrap about your own favorites or someone else's.

Lia's favorite things are always changing, but I wanted to record her favorites at the moment. Instead of trying to take pictures of all of Lia's favorite things, I took a few pictures and labeled them, then I listed the rest of the favorites. This simplified the page and allowed me to include only pictures that I really loved.

Jill Hornby

I listed each of my favorite things right this minute in random order. I wanted documentation of what my favorite things are right now, this second in my life. I would love it if my mom had kept something like this so I could know what her favorite things were at age 27. I didn't write the list ahead of time; I just sat down and wrote it right from my heart.

Meghan Heath Dymock

For this Dare, I knew I wanted to do pictures of Chloe, but I have so many favorites. So I made a mini book to showcase all my favorite shots of our sweet little pup. Since every picture was of Chloe, I wanted the book itself to be very interesting. I constructed each page by hand out of various elements. Some are made of photos, others of envelopes and even a plastic package.

Kristina Contes

It just warms my flippin' heart how much Tyler loves this little camera—so that's what I had to scrap for this Dare. I wanted the photos to be the focus of this layout— Tyler and the camera kind of say it all. So I placed them centered toward the top. I chose colors that picked up on the colors from the photos—which happened to be complementary (blue and orange), which is always good times.

Nisa Fiin

BLING: *Who doesn't love it? Makes life a little bit fancier. Bling has always been a great way to dress up an outfit, and now it's a great way to dress up your scrapbook pages as well! Create a page using glitter, rhinestones, sparkle, etc. Bling it out. You know you wanna.*

The first thing I thought of when I heard the Bling Dare was to make a glitter K. I covered a chipboard monogram, added some wings, sparkly ribbon, Swarovski crystals and a cool quote...perfect.

Kristina Contes

I had been wanting for some time to do a page about how my wedding rings were stolen. This was the Dare to do it for. I used the rhinestones just as an accent, but once you read the journaling, you'll know their meaning on the page. This photo is one of my favorites because it just shows us walking down the aisle. I don't think this page screams, "Sad story ahead," and I didn't want it to.

Laura Kurz

once in a blue moon i let my mama give me

CUTE hAIR

I wanted to do a girly page for this Dare since I don't scrap "girly" that often. This was so much fun, I decided to go all out and use rhinestones and sparkles. The photo I used suited this layout perfectly since at that time, Sophie didn't do girly all that often either. It was a rare occasion that Sophie would let Rhi make her hair pretty. To bring it all together, I made one big bling explosion!

Genevieve Simmonds

This Dare was fun for me because I love rhinestones! But this page was also very therapeutic for me because I was having a difficult time artistically. I made this page with the intention of being free with my art. I wrote all over the photos, added rhinestones, tape and anything else I wanted. I did not restrict myself with this page whatsoever, and I love how being free with my art allowed me to tap back into my creativity.

Meghan Heath Dymock

WHERE I GREW UP:

Where did you grow up? Like, actually grow up... it could be a physical place, or a time when you or your child came of age. This is your opportunity to take an inventory of your life and establish where you are, where you came from, or where you hope to go. Scrap it.

trans ATLANTIC

I don't come from anywhere. No hometown. No place I come back to. I was born somewhere. I went to school a lot of other places. Now I live somewhere else. For some reason my clearest memory of early childhood is sleeping on the floor of the flight American used to operate from Tampa to London. I remember so many airplanes. There used to be decks of cards. There used to be a dress code. There were seats that faced each other in groups of four. There were air-pockets and ashtrays. I have no accent. No regional colloquialisms. My point of reference, the thing I share with people, seems to be air travel in the 1980s.

I've never had a hometown. When people ask me where I'm from, I haven't the slightest idea what to tell them. My family did a lot of moving around. What I remember best growing up are airplanes and strange places.

Alison Flynn

1977 another time another place

Feels like it anyway. The seventies, when the most high-tech gadget in the house was the eight-track player and nobody thought to put bike helmets on their kids. We had less stuff, but sometimes I feel like we had more of what's important. More running around, outside. More days spent at the library with Mom. More playing make-believe and dress-up. More picnics on fall weekends. We didn't have a huge inflatable snowman in our front yard but we had an advent wreath. We didn't have video games but we had neighborhood-wide games of Star Wars complete with invented action and dialogue. We didn't have HDTV but we had nightly dance "concerts" with costumes and a flashlight "spotlight." We didn't have computers but we had crayons and little bits of paper that could be turned into wonderful things. We didn't feel afraid to step out of our yards, we felt free to run all over the neighborhood. We were happy and active and imaginative and carefree. At least, that's how I remember it. I'm thankful for what I didn't have growing up. When I think of that time, it all seems idyllic and picture-perfect. I know it was neither. But in my mind, the hard parts melt away. The world was wonderful.

I interpreted the "where I grew up" Dare as a time period rather than a place. I wanted to capture some of my feelings about growing up in the seventies. I remember my early childhood being simple and happy and safe, and that's the lens through which I view that time period. I hope that's the impression that comes through in my layout.

Anja Wade

I created this page to celebrate the city where I grew up. The photo was taken while I was out for dinner with my mum and sisters, experimenting with my camera. I thought the picture was so "my city," with the person walking by, the taxi, the multi-colored lights and the foliage at the forefront. This page developed in an organic way very quickly, with all the inspiration derived from the picture.

Genevieve Simmonds

I remember jumping from the stairs, getting a running start through the hallway, and sliding to a stop on the hardwood floors. I remember the vines in the forest and how we used to swing on them for hours. I remember dad putting together the desk for my bedroom and cursing. I remember waiting for my first date in the living room, seeing his headlights slowly creep up our street and into our driveway. I remember running my hand across the wood panels on the stairs. I remember my first high school party. A classmate asked me if he could bring beer and I thought I was going to die, right there, on the spot. I remember Pop Pop arriving for Christmas and Thanksgiving with bags of apples in his trunk. I remember lip-synching to Carney Wilson in the basement with the Soolier twins. I remember playing "The Thinking Game" in high school with Jenny, Jen, and Asheley. We thought we knew so much about life and what it would hold for us. I remember opening the door to a flower delivery from my coworkers the day after cousin Lisa died. I remember waiting for the school bus and us always having our hands up in the air to keep the gnats at bay. I remember skateboarding down our steep driveway, and then sledding down it during the snow. I remember mom's short-lived flower garden on the side hill. I remember hitting mom's car mirror against the side of the garage not long after my 16th birthday. I remember summer dinners on the screened-in porch. I remember how much I loved turning left onto Shadow Lane returning home during college breaks. I remember Halloween on Shadow Lane. There weren't a lot of houses, but everyone knew you. And you felt safe. Always. I remember gripper and fiercer – the birds that came every spring and left every fall and always had that same call, "Gripper! Fiercer!" I remember sleeping with the windows open and only hearing the crickets. I remember dad's leather recliner. I remember the great climbing tree in the backyard, just up the hill.

When people ask where I grew up, I usually tell them the name of the town I lived in, from age 6-17... But the truth is – I grew up here. At Sugar Creek Camp. Middle of nowhere and beyond gorgeous. The summer I turned 18... on my own for the first time. Surrounded by trees and water and amazing people... This is where I really grew up...

• SUGAR CREEK CAMP 1997 • I GREW UP IN THESE WOODS •

Not normal

dYSFUNCTiONAL LOVE

STRENGTH HAS A MILLION FACES

My Childhood was far from normal. But it's all I have & it made me who I am today.

I don't have a lot of great photos of the house I grew up in, but I love this photo of the front steps. It reminds me of what I loved most about this house—how inviting it was! I had 13 years of memories to document, so I made the type small (but readable) and bolded every other memory to make them distinct from each other.

Laura Kurz

Though I was born and raised in small town Wisconsin, I really grew up—like actually *grew* up—at camp. I used products on this page that complemented the "outdoor" colors of the photo. And to physically bring in some of the outdoors, I added some bits of grape vine.

Nisa Fiin

Instead of interpreting this Dare as a physical place I grew up, I showed *how* I grew up. I come from a rather bizarre family of divorce and half siblings, which made for a wonderful experience as a child. But not knowing where I fit was rough. Luckily it taught me to be fiercely independent and self-sufficient. I'm not proud of our family, but I do love each member very much. They all played a part in shaping the person I am today, even if it wasn't in the traditional way. I used a collage of images to show happy and sad times.

Kristina Contes

ACCOMPLISHMENTS:

Big or small, our lives are full of accomplishments. Starting a business, earning a degree, following your dreams...goals you have set and reached. Sometimes just getting out of bed in the morning is a major accomplishment. Scrap about your journey to get there or how great it felt to finally make it.

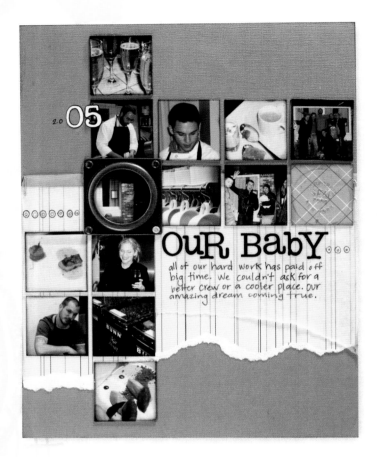

My husband and I own a restaurant, so naturally I knew that would be the topic of my page for this Dare. I used a collage of different restaurant shots to show all the little details and people that have helped along the way.

Kristina Contes

It has really been an accomplishment to make it on any vacation after having a kid. This is a photo from the first vacation we've been on in about four years.

Linda Buranasakorn

I am so proud of how much my husband and I have accomplished since we have been married. We both have earned our bachelor's degrees, and he is currently earning two master's degrees! We have owned one home in Utah and are now living in our second home in Arizona. We have been able to conquer hardships and understand each other now more than ever before. I am very proud of how hard we have both worked for these accomplishments.

Meghan Heath Dymock

For this Dare, there was no doubt in my mind that I had to scrap my brother. That boy is king of accomplishments, not the least of which was graduating from Boot Camp. I wanted the photos to be the central part of this layout. The page needed journaling, but I wanted it to be secondary to the photos, so I wrapped it around the outside, to require the reader to get involved in the page in order to read it. You can't just glance and read the story. It requires a little effort.

Nisa Fiin

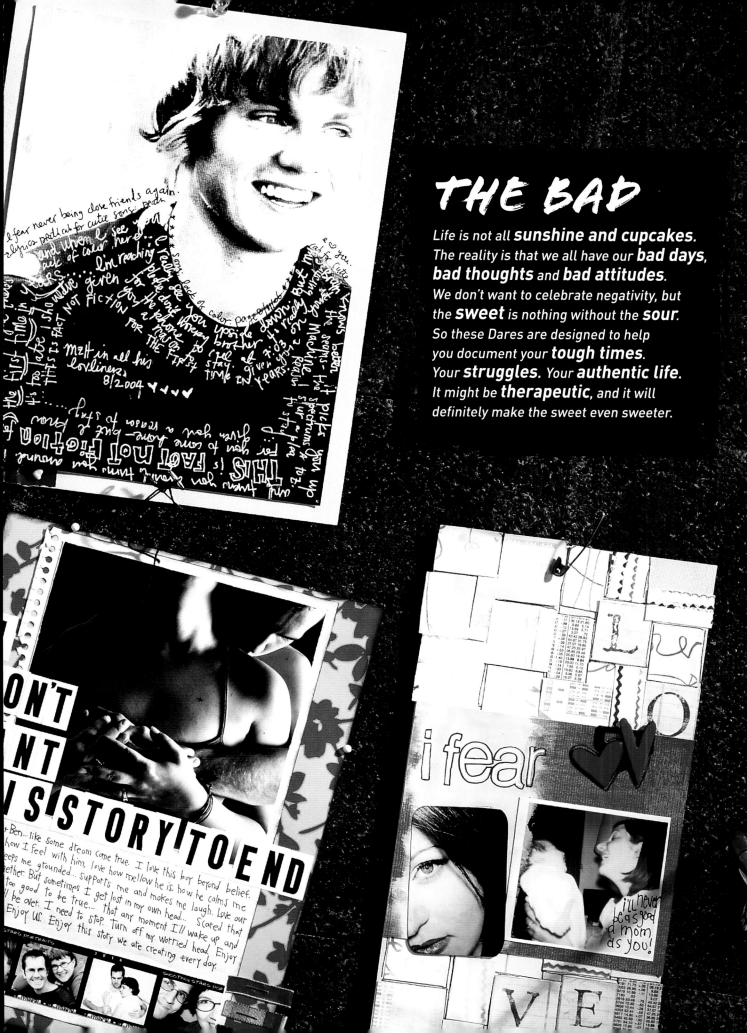

THE BAD

Life is not all **sunshine and cupcakes**.
The reality is that we all have our **bad days**,
bad thoughts and **bad attitudes**.
We don't want to celebrate negativity, but
the **sweet** is nothing without the **sour**.
So these Dares are designed to help
you document your **tough times**.
Your **struggles**. Your **authentic life**.
It might be **therapeutic**, and it will
definitely make the sweet even sweeter.

HARD: *We've all been through a lot at one time or another. Learning experiences, tough situations, major life lessons. It can be just like therapy to scrap the hard times... .get it out, get it on paper. These pages aren't the easiest to make, but we all agree that making them will help you grow and learn. So scrap something you find hard.*

I wanted to make it clear that I have a lot to say about my parents' recent separation, but I don't want it to be all out there. I put the photo over the journaling and attached it on the right side with staples. The journaling can be read in full by lifting the photo.

Genevieve Simmonds

There are so many things in life that are hard. If I thought about it, I could come up with at least six pages about hard stuff. Then I realized that the one thing that makes all the hard things ten times worse is my anxiety. So the hardest thing of all is to just chill. If I could just relax, all the other tough stuff wouldn't seem so bad.

Kristina Contes

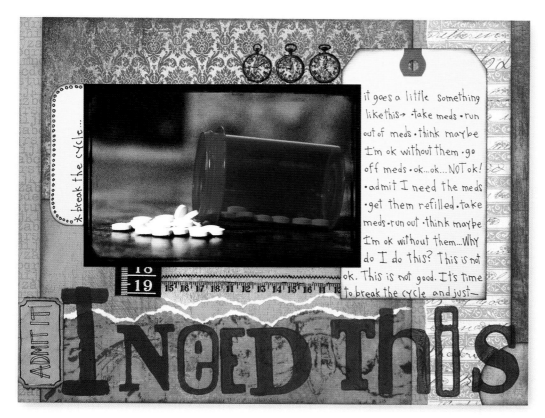

it goes a little something like this→ •take meds •run out of meds •think maybe I'm ok without them •go off meds •ok...ok... NOT ok! •admit I need the meds •get them refilled •take meds •run out •think maybe I'm ok without them...Why do I do this? This is not ok. This is not good. It's time to break the cycle and just—

* break the cycle...

ADMIT IT

For this Dare, I wanted to really dig deep...scrap something I struggle with. And this is it: accepting that I need these meds. Making this layout was pretty therapeutic...it was good to get it down and force myself to admit this. I used a variety of alphabet stamps and patterned papers, kind of crazy in the background, to illustrate how chaotic things get when I'm not taking these meds like I should.

Nisa Fiin

For this Dare, I instantly thought of my sister. Aubrie is a perfectionist down to her core who was having a hard time with the changes taking place in her life. I wanted to convey to her that she needs to open her eyes and see herself and how amazing she is because sometimes she doesn't see it!

Meghan Heath Dymock

ajh

OPEN YOUR EYES

EXPECTATION

You Are Not Here

You Are Here

and see you for the first time

GUILTY PLEASURES: These are the things we love, but know we shouldn't. Sometimes we sneak around with a copy of a trashy tabloid or spend too much money at the mall or obsess over a certain rock star. Identify your guilty pleasure and create a layout that pays homage to that thing you love...even though you shouldn't.

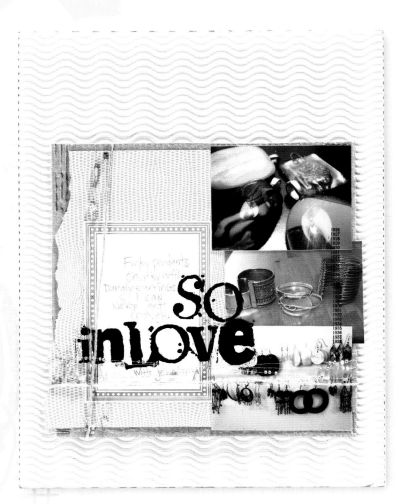

I have so many guilty pleasures, but one that is a bit of a problem is jewelry. I am constantly buying a new ring or a cool bracelet. For this Dare, I took photos of my different jewelry collections and journaled about my obsession. I used beads and wire to give the page a jeweled feel. Since my collection is a mix of expensive pieces and flea market finds, I decided to throw in some hemp rope to show the contrast of my collection.

Kristina Contes

It took me a while to come up with a topic for this Dare, but as I was thinking, I constantly came back to food (bread and cheese, in particular) and nice red wine. I wanted a photo featuring my yummy guilty pleasures all at once. So I purchased a huge chunk of Brie ("I need it"), some French bread, and, well, the red wine was on hand. Once the photo was shot, the rest fell into place quite nicely.

Genevieve Simmonds

This Dare made me think about how I am constantly taking photographs! Photography is definitely a guilty pleasure for me because often I don't stop to enjoy the moment, I just take a large amount of photos of the moment. This page was inspired by this photo that I didn't know my dad was taking as I took photos of my sister. To make the page fun, I added different colors of letter stickers and the M rub-on to my wrist along with the gemstones.

Meghan Heath Dymock

MAC makeup is easily one of my favorite pleasures. I go into the store, my face lights up, and I have to run right up and see what the new limited edition eye colors are. As soon as the idea of making this page for this Dare popped into my head, I also got the idea to take a picture of my brushes, then individually cut them out to use as a border. Then I took a picture of a bunch of the makeup in a pile. (Keep in mind it's only like a third of my stash. Yikes.) I blew up one for the border and kept one smaller to use on the body of the page. If I thought it would have stayed and wasn't so wasteful, I would have put makeup on the actual page.

Jamie Bagley

FEAR: *The world is full of scary stuff. What's your fear? Maybe you're afraid of the ceiling falling down or eating a spider in your sleep. Maybe you worry about money or your health or your children's safety. Scrap a page about one of your biggest fears. Sometimes when you get it out, it becomes a teensy bit more manageable.*

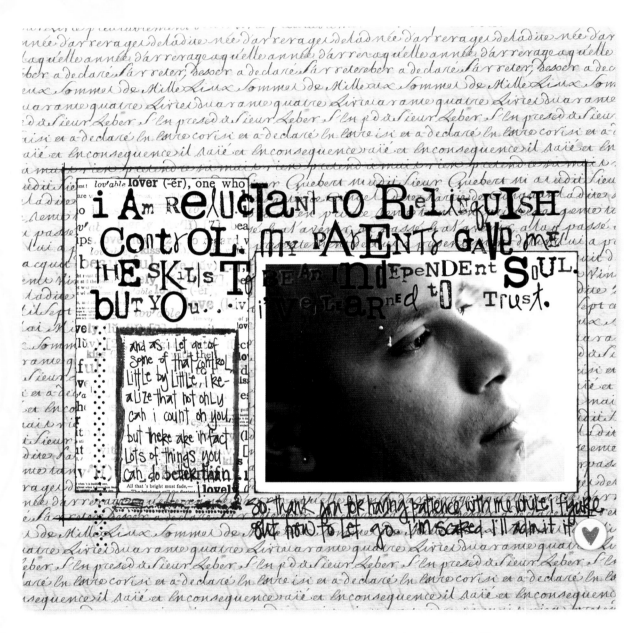

I wanted my husband to know one of the important changes he's made in my life. It's a pretty unique feeling for me to rely on someone. I realize more and more over the years that it helps me to be able to trust Dren, and it makes him feel good, too. Super important.

Genevieve Simmonds

I took this photo of my brother Zack at a summer picnic when he was joking around with our family. When I uploaded it to my computer, I started crying because it is the most beautiful photo of him I have ever taken. Our relationship has been strained lately, and I fear we will never be close again. I miss our friendship, our talks and our jokes. The journaling is song lyrics for "Lack of Color" by Death Cab for Cutie.

Meghan Heath Dymock

These days it seems all my fears are somehow related to the restaurant we own. Will it be a success? Will people like it? Will people "get" it? The restaurant is a huge undertaking, and I worry every day about whether we did the right thing. But as long as we stay true to our vision, we will succeed.

Kristina Contes

no one told me

that motherhood
would bring about so many

fears

I fear those
who would cause harm to others.
I fear the horrible things
that are happening in the world today.
I fear disease.
I fear losing you.
I am afraid of what might happen
when you are out of my sight.
I am afraid of doing the wrong thing
as your mother.
I fear not being able to protect you.
But I will always try.

Ask me what my fears are, and I can tell you that many—most—of them relate to my children. It wasn't very hard to think about the things that worry me most. On this page I mentioned my biggest fears, but I ended my journaling hopeful, with the thought that those fears can never overwhelm me because my need to protect my children is so great. This page was meant for my children to see, and when they are able to understand it, I hope it lets them know how deeply I care for them and how important they are to me.

Michelle Guray

For this layout, I wanted to get my journaling out and still keep it light but a little serious. And I just really wanted to communicate how much I love my mom.

Sarah Bowen

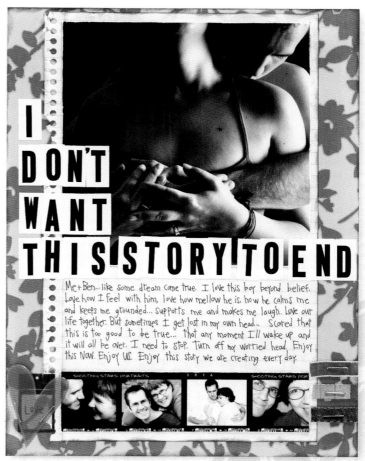

I'm scared of lots of random things: owls, kidney stones, being chased. But my biggest fear is that something will happen and Ben and I will end. Honestly, nothing scares me more.... I used a background paper that is pink and red, to reinforce the warmth and love in the photos. I used similarly colored accents to enhance this feel. I used a striking, slightly intimate photograph as the main photo, along with notebook paper—as though you're getting a private glimpse into a diary entry.

Nisa Fiin

FIGHTS:

Arguments, spats and disagreements you have gone through. Sometimes you make up, sometimes it's over and you hate them forever. Either way, you learn and grow from these experiences. Scrap it—it will help you understand these rough patches and bring perspective to the choices you have made.

STILL FIGHTING IT

Before You, I was living some mad drama. ex-boy and I fought all the time. like ALL the time. everything was a fight. everything was yelling, screaming, crying... everyday I lived that for almost three years...
With You everything is different. We talk. we listen. we work it out. it's all good. But that shadow of what was still haunts my head. I lived that drama so intensely... it's hard to let it go. I have to remind myself not to freak out, not to push you to fight. I'm getting better. everytime we work through something else I am reminded → this is good. this is different. That shadow still lingers. But I'm still fighting it...

Honestly, I struggled with scrapping this Dare, as I really don't fight with people these days. But I realized that for me, the fight is an internal one. Because of past relationships, I struggle with not pushing things to the point of fighting with others. So technically the fight is to realize that this relationship is different, this is good. Fighting the past; fighting to keep it there.

Nisa Fiin

I have fought with so many people in my life, I didn't know which fight to document. But I realized I fight with all my best friends, and I wanted to document that! I picked photos of my best friends who I fight with once a year or a bit more. I think there is something in my soul that likes fighting. The main photo is one my sister took of me when I was in a fight at dinner. I think fighting is good for everyone once in awhile and actually seems to strengthen my bond with everyone.

Meghan Heath Dymock

if you can't fight with me, we can't be best friends

it's true. I am confrontational. fighting has never bothered me - actually I sort of like it - in a weird way. ... every friend I have that I am close to I fight with at least once a year. I can't be best friends with anyone who can't hold their own with me - not physically! But an actual verbal altercation seems to really work for me and my friendships! of course with fights come making up time. maybe that is part of the connection! go fights! ♥ ♥ ♥

When I think of Cheryl I often become scared. She's one of those girls that has always been in my life. Some years we are inseparable, others we don't speak at all. Right now is one of those distant phases, and I miss her so much. As I get older, I worry that this time may be the last. That she won't pick up the phone and say "What up bi-otch!?" like she always has. I am scared that this will be our last disagreement. That we will no longer be best friends. That we have grown apart for good. This relationship has taught me that you need to tell your friends how special they are, no matter how badly you may want to kill them. They are what is real and you need to hold on to that no matter what.

Though I've gotten into plenty of random fights in my life, a particular lapse in communication has really stood out in my mind. I decided to create a page about my friend Cheryl. I found an old photo booth picture of Cheryl and me. I journaled about how I am scared that this fight may have been our last.

Kristina Contes

The day I chose to work on this Dare, Jaxon was testing boundaries and being stubborn. Sometimes these interactions do feel like arguments even though they shouldn't. We're parents. But we're still human beings, and we do second-guess ourselves. Feeling that we're fighting helps bring me back to the calm and rational parent role.

Genevieve Simmonds

A boy's will is the wind's will.

we hate fighting with you. it feels like a fight because you're so smart... you're a part of the conversation. it can't be a democracy... we don't want it to be a dictatorship. oh yeah... it's called parenting. sometimes it feels like a fight.

REGRETS: *We all have 'em. What is something you regret? Something you would take back in a second if you could...an unfinished chapter that needs closure. Create a layout about it and let the page be that closure.*

This is so it-classic early me taking a picture of early you. You leaned down to tie your shoe and I snapped a shot real quick. Sneaky. I wish I would have taken so many more photos of you in the beginning...of us in the beginning. Pictures of you showing up on my doorstep late Friday night after driving 7 hours so we could be together for a while. You hanging out in my little apartment- that would become our little apartment. Just you & me being-in the beginning of it all. I am such a picture person- but I was afraid the camera would scare you off. The click of the shutter would break the spell of you & me. I try to live my life with no regrets, But I will admit I regret this. In the beginning, I took too few photos of you.

I try to live my life without regrets—everything is a learning experience after all. But I do regret not taking more photos of Ben in the beginning of us. Somehow I thought taking photos of Ben would scare him away...so I had to sneak shots! I used bright colors for the ribbon, paper and rub-ons because, though it is a page about regrets, it's kind of silly as far as regrets go.

Nisa Fiin

i Wish foR mOre

i wish i had been able to stay home with you for longer.. i feel like i missed out. but it all probably worked out for the best. funny thing, redret. funny thing!

This was a difficult topic to broach, so I wanted to do a page that was pretty, with lots of detail, to balance the somewhat heavy subject matter. I used scallop deco scissors on the photos, vinyl sleeve, and a journaling block as a "pretty" touch, along with fabric, stitching and buttons. The photos are so Jaxon, so boy. I love the contrast between the elements, and they also come together so well to tell the story.

Genevieve Simmonds

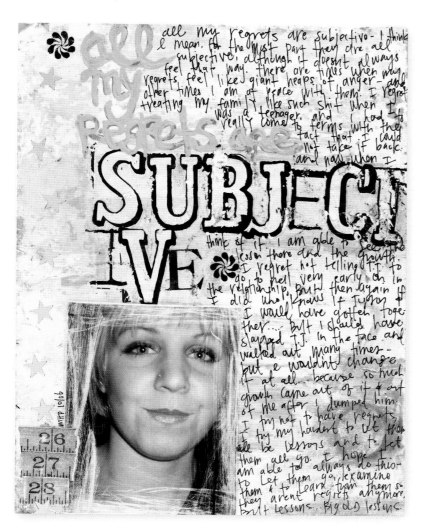

all my regrets are subjective - I think I mean. for the most part they are all subjective, although it doesn't always feel that way. there are times when my regrets feel like giant heaps of anger - and other times I am at peace with them. I regret treating my family like such shit when I was a teenager. and I really come to terms with the fact that I could not take if back. and now when I think if I am able to see the lesson there and the growth I regret not telling T.J. to go to hell very early on in the relationship. But then again if I did who knows if Tyler & I would have gotten together... But I should have stayed T.J. in the face and walked out many times - but I wouldn't change it at all... because so much growth came out of it & out of me after I dumped him. I try not to have regrets. I try my hardest to let them all be lessons and to let them all go. I hope I am able to always do this - to let them go, examine them & to learn from them so they aren't regrets anymore, but lessons. Big old lessons.

SUBJECTIVE

I wanted the journaling to be the main focus because I had so much to say about all my regrets! I try to learn from my regrets and having a page documenting them seemed magical to me. I sanded the photograph after getting it wet and painted the white cardstock with gold paint and a splash of pink paint. The 26, 27 and 28 stickers symbolize the past, present and future and all the lessons I still have to learn so I don't end up with more regrets.

Meghan Heath Dymock

If I sit down and think about it, there are key points in my life that I thought I regretted. In actuality they were just choices and turns of events that led me to where I am today. A recent turning point in my life was when I dropped out of FIT. It was around the time Jonathan and I were first dating. I always wonder what my life would have been like if I had stayed...but now I know that it was for the best. We're married and we own a restaurant, which is amazing. Plus I've found a new way to nurture my creativity: scrapbooking. So it was meant to be that I am an art school drop out.

Kristina Contes

I still can't believe I dropped out of FIT. Jewelry design has always been a huge interest of mine. I guess everything happened for a reason because now I have found scrap booking, and I don't have to take the Long Island Rail Road into Penn to do it. So I guess I am OK with being an art school drop out.

ART SCHOOL DROP OUT

MAKE A MESS:
Roll up those sleeves, it's time to make a mess. Bust out the paints, alcohol inks and gessoes. Create something out of the ordinary and make it soulful. Let your inner artist out for a run. Play. Get dirty. It's good for you every once in a while.

Photos Reborn

For this Dare, I busted out the gel medium and paints, rolled up my sleeves and went to town. I printed the cyanotype photo from an antique negative and some sun print paper. To do this, lay the negative over the paper and expose it to the sun for a few minutes, until the exposed paper turns nearly white. Bring it back inside and dip it in a pan of water. The water will reverse the image (to create a positive) and will also stop the chemical process and set the photo. I made an antiqued background with an old text book and paint to balance the look of old and new...the negatives are old, but they are given new life in my printing.

Nisa Fiin

In this page I tried to portray the excitement of the fountains. I just went crazy with the paint, using a brush to spatter, smudge, and smear paint across the page. I felt like the paint helped show how exciting the fountains were.

Jill Hornby

I knew this Dare was regarding the look of the page, but it made me think of a messy topic, too. In this case, it was a time in my life that I spent with one of my ex-boyfriends. It was partially him and our drama and partially my lifestyle at that time, but it was very chaotic, very crazy, and yes, messy. To get my page "messy," I hand-painted the buildings, used torn cardboard, painted all over the edges and on top of the photos, tore my patterned paper and used patterned paper that had a distressed pattern.

Jessica Fulkerson

My thought process went from mess = paint = artist = expression = tattoos. Thus, my page was born. I used various photos of my ink and piercings to show that I have plenty, and they are part of who I am. Most people say, "You have such a pretty face, but then there are all these spikes everywhere." I see these as little diamonds, so I added the crystals to the right side to show that body art doesn't have to be rough and tough. My ethereal painting and color choices support that idea. Plus, you know how I love juxtaposition!

Kristina Contes

Looking back on my time with Vince is bittersweet. I don't miss us and our drama and I don't really miss him. I do have fond memories of that time though. Carefree, crazy partying, the whole BnO crew, flying down the 101 for a show on Sunset at a seconds notice, nonstop energy, a total adventure. It wasn't hard to see that going like that couldn't last for long. Us, L.A., maybe even a part of myself. it all blew up, fizzled out, faded away. And I'm ok with that...

We burnt that city down.

time's up

THE WORST THING

THE UGLY

These are the things you really don't want to scrap. The ones you'd rather **forget**, **tuck away** at the back of a drawer and **never think about again**. There's no need to dwell on these things, but it helps to examine them rather than stuff them away. We encourage you to **look inside yourself** and **conquer your demons**. Face the ugly truth and beat it to the ground. A bit of scrap therapy. Give it a try. It feels oh so good to **let it all out**.

2 1 34 30
IN MY

28 29 30 31 1 INCH
these are all bad numbers!

Can be cranky. Bitchy. extremely insecure. some one who complains about the many injustice in this world. I often feel that I am doomed to live a life of bitterness and depression. I an constantly reliving things that have happene in the past. Constantly having bouts of negativit Feeling like shit. But you know what? When I'm on, I'm ON. No one Laughs as rediculously as I do. No one Loves the way I do. No one gives their heart as much as I do. No one gets it like I do. So even though I can be a bit of a mess and a total drama Queen, the Good stuff seriously outweighs the bad. I am vibrant and honest. I wear my heart, brain & soul on my shoulder. I am entirely unique & entirely amazing. True

me.

AD...

see... there are good
ers and bad numbers.
t sure if you're aware.
attle in my head. It's
onstant. Seeking out
mbers and avoiding
s not rational. I know.
there. In my
lways.

66

I am intolerant.
and critical.
and pissy.

I get annoyed.
and bitchy.
and sharp at
the edges.

I withdraw.
I roll my eyes.
I can hear it
in my voice.

I am the Ice Queen.

The worst part.
I do it to the
people I love most.

12 20 6 T.L.J.
THE WORST THING
I couldn't save you!

to know I couldn't The worst
Love at age 15 took save you
we laugh and cry a
our relationship and the
spent with you and I
addict. It started
an early age. I
would continue on to a more addicted future. I didn't
know you would become entangled into a life filled
with heroin and needles and track marks all over
your body. I still love you with a piece of it all over
I never

thing is that
I'm still wanting
still loves me. My first
breath away made
Lot I look back of
four years of my life
can see you there - the
developing at such
did not know you

*TLJ

defining moment

IMPERFECT PHOTO:
*Now is the time to pull out those flubs.
Those shots you never thought you'd scrap...those grainy, out of focus,
poorly cropped, bad pictures. Photos don't have to be perfect to tell a story.
Sometimes in their imperfection, they manage to get it just right.
Scrap an imperfect photo.*

For this Dare, I used a blurry photo of my brother playing
bass with his band; he moves around so much, it's hard to
get a clear one. But I love the way this one came out after
adjusting the color and brightness a bit in Photoshop;
it reminds me of a painting.

Anja Wade

ALEY GOT US HOOKED ON THE JOYCAM IT WAS SO FUN!

these baby polaroids were a part of every social gathering for quite a while. the instant gratification of a moment in time captured is so great. aley & me, rhi & me. 2001(ish).

So often I will go through photos from a particular event and be unhappy with the quality. But usually even those pictures convey the memory, bringing back emotions, feelings and thoughts. I wanted to make a page reflecting the fun we had with the Joycam, as well as these two favorite shots of me and my sisters.

Genevieve Simmonds

Summer flew by in a blur of phone calls, parties and sunset afternoons. In my mind... it was just one long conversation interrupted only by work, location changes and drink refills. Always too much to say and too little time.

I've always loved this photo for its great colors and movement, and this Dare was the perfect opportunity to use it. And it works, capturing that moment in time, as the summer flew by in a blur.

Jamaica Edgell

With an active little pup, it's easy to take bad pictures! I created my own patterned paper background with all her different nicknames to encompass a broad range of photos without any one topic. Just a big old homage to our dog who we love very much.

Kristina Contes

My parents don't like to have their photos published anywhere! When their photo appears on a page I have published or posted online, I always cover their eyes, even when the photo is cute, like this one. The journaling is about how my parents like their privacy, but I also included the story of how they met and traits of theirs I admire.

Meghan Heath Dymock

ok, So-I'm not fully IN the picture... But this is still one of my favorite photos of me. So happy + hanging out with you, my small friend. Plus, you helped take this photo - LOVE that. Love how much you love cameras & taking crazy pics with me. Love how we have a blast no matter what we do on our days together... playing, talking (babbling), laughing... It's all good. I'm telling you, TY. little you + me... we just CLICK. Yup. That's it. (love you.)

CliCK

I love imperfect photos—sometimes they are seriously the best. I love this photo of Tyler and me, even if I'm only partly in the photo. It's my smile in this shot that's the important part. Since this photo was black and white, I had free reign over color choices, so I used yellows, greens and blue as the background and orange to make the title pop.

Nisa Fiin

My friend had the most gorgeous wedding, and thankfully I wasn't the wedding photographer, because I did a really bad job in the church. Some of my photos did turn out great, but I had really wanted to scrap this photo of them walking down the aisle after exchanging their vows. You can just barely see the beautiful colors of her bouquet.

Laura Kurz

BEAUTIFUL WEDDING
BAD PHOTOGRAPHER

October 14, 2006
Carron and Ben DeGrass

DISTRESS:

Create a layout that heavily showcases distressing... sanding, ripping, painting. Get gritty. Get grimy. Don't worry about looking pretty. Let go. Dig in. Create and experiment with new mediums. Yeah, baby, we like it raw.

There is something so satisfying about seriously distressing a layout—really getting in there with some sandpaper and elbow grease. On this layout I sanded the background paper like mad. For the photos, I laid them down on my cutting mat with one edge slightly extended past the edge of the photo. Then I sanded that side, so I got a double line of distressing.

Nisa Fiin

I found this survey in a magazine and decided to use it in this layout. After laying pieces of masking tape over the patterned paper, I rubbed them with a brown ink pad. I distressed the star stickers, too, by sanding them.

Jamie Bagley

I love this photo of the old door with peeling paint and rusted metal, and I wanted to mimic that feel in the layout. I junked up the layout with paint, staples, tape and walnut ink. For the title, I used letter stickers, chalked over them and then removed a few of the stickers.

Sarah Bowen

I sanded all of my photos to give the edges a rough appearance. I created my own patterned background paper with a stamp that I used with distress embossing powder and repeated until the page was covered. I inked the edges of my journaling and crinkled up my letter stickers. Then I stapled it onto a piece of corrugated cardboard. I distressed it every step of the way and loved every minute of it. Distressing rules. As does my wonderful husband.

Kristina Contes

THE WORST THING:
Most people don't broadcast it, but we all struggle with it. That little something about yourself that you just hate. Something you are ashamed of. Something you cringe over. Create a page about it. Maybe this is your chance to change it, to move past it and make yourself the person you want to be.

You see... there are good numbers and bad numbers. I'm not sure if you're aware. They battle in my head. It's near constant. Seeking out good numbers and avoiding bad. It's not rational, I know. But it's there. In my head. Always.

For this Dare, I scrapped about my obsession with numbers. My head is always over-analyzing and obsessing about them—drives me crazy. I covered a whole piece of paper with signage number stickers and then cut out part of a circle to frame the photo and lead your eye around the layout. I laid it over a piece of paper that I printed a variety of numbers on. I also chose additional accents that showcased numbers—the ruler paper, the tape measure tape and the number rub-ons.

Nisa Fiin

I have an ex-boyfriend who I tried to save from a life of addiction. I couldn't save him, but in the process I saved myself. I wanted this page to be dramatic, so I chose a black background with an exaggerated photo of myself. I journaled all over the photo except on my hands because I wanted the focus to be on my hands praying for him, as I still do.

Meghan Heath Dymock

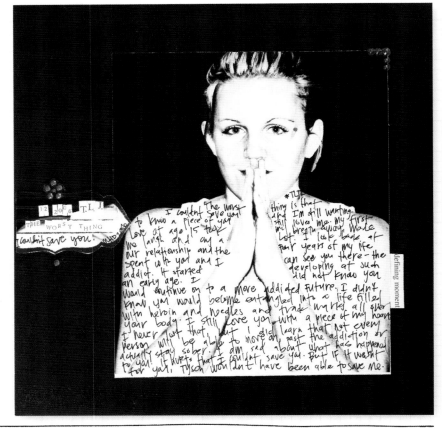

I am intolerant.
and critical.
and pissy.

I get annoyed.
and bitchy.
and sharp at
the edges.

I withdraw.
I roll my eyes.
I can hear it
in my voice.

I am the Ice Queen.

The worst part.
I do it to the
people I love most.

As a teenager, my snooty attitude toward my mom and her friends earned me the nickname the Ice Queen. Unfortunately, as I've gotten older, some of those habits remain. And they are my worst habits. I added iridescent sequins to the layout to sparkle just a tiny bit like snowflakes.

Jamaica Edgell

This Dare was to journal about the worst thing about yourself—no problem for me! I used an outtake from a recent photo shoot and journaled on the white space.

Kristina Contes

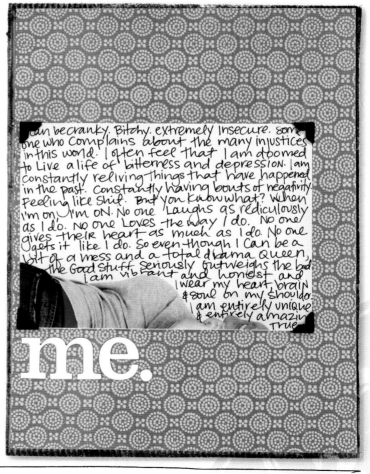

me.

I can be cranky. Bitchy. extremely Insecure. someone who complains about the many injustices in this world. I often feel that I am doomed to live a life of bitterness and depression. I am constantly reliving things that have happened in the past. Constantly having bouts of negativity. Feeling like shit. But you know what? When I'm on, I'm ON. No one laughs as rediculously as I do. No one loves the way I do. No one gives their heart as much as I do. No one gets it like I do. So even though I can be a bit of a mess and a total drama Queen, the Good stuff seriously outweighs the bad. I am vibrant and honest and I wear my heart, brain & soul on my shoulder. I am entirely unique & entirely amazing. True.

PISSED OFF:

Temper tantrums, things you hate, things that make you angry. Every once in a while it's just so great to scream and yell and hate the world for one reason or another. What pisses you off? Get mad. Get real. Get brutally honest. Make a layout about what really boils your blood.

I knew right away I wanted to do a page about President Bush and my disgust with our current administration. It's the only thing that really gets my blood boiling. At first I wrote a very eloquent statement about why I disagreed with many current decisions, but then I remembered the Dare was "Pissed Off!," so I let loose. It was a great emotional release. While others may not agree with my opinions, I hope they are inspired either to get as free as I let myself get or at least to journal about their own political beliefs. Pages like this will be amazing to look back on down the road.

Jessica Fulkerson

I have plenty of material for this Dare, that's for sure. Since I'd rather not have a giant rant as the focal point of my layout, I decided to create little string and button envelopes to house all my thoughts. The stickers on the side give a warning that I'm really going to go off. The dictionary clipping of angry also ties in to the pissed off theme.

Kristina Contes

she gets bent.

i will
admit,
i get a
teeny bit
bent when
i can see
an open
cupboard
door out of
the corner
of my eye.
quirky quirky
but i can't
stand it!

I tackled this page after coming off some "heavier" Dares, so I didn't really feel like thinking about things that piss me off. So I put a humorous spin on it instead, although open cupboard doors do irritate me. Every time I look at this page now it's almost like torture!

Genevieve Simmonds

I wanted to create a page that tells the story of how I get pissed off before I get sad or depressed. I can remember being a child and finding myself angry before being sad. I inked the bottom corner of the page with walnut ink and then added wax drippings. I added the photo and then the journaling. The golden flowers were a gift from my sister.

Meghan Heath Dymock

pissed off finds me first. infuriated and mad screaming and hating everyone before I am hysterical crying in a heap on the floor

It has been this way always.

MORTIFIED:

Eeek. These pages are all about the completely embarrassing. The time you had your skirt stuck in your undies or tripped in front of a room full of people. Yes, it's embarrassing but hysterical when you realize it happens to the best of us. Get it down and then laugh at yourself just as hard as everybody else did.

I'm pretty sure that one day soon you'LL be embarrassed by this photo, but until then we can have a giggle.

I left this Dare for last because I couldn't find any photos of me smiling with my brace face or with my boy haircut. But then I found this photo of Little T with yogurt all over her face. It made me smile and reminded me of "the yogurt incident" from the other day (a different yogurt incident). These are the stories that we are totally going to harass our children about later in life. Hee hee.

Genevieve Simmonds

This scrap subject is *so* much fun! Mortification in retrospect is always funny. This is the kind of picture I hope to include in my niece's slide show at her wedding to make her blush and everyone laugh. This kind of picture is also fun to take because of the disapproving stares and giggles you get from people watching you take this picture. Plus it's always fun to have pictures embarrassing someone else rather than yourself, right?

Jamie Bagley

i see you!

sometimes its the littlest things. Like looking back on moments like this & cracking up. summer 06

Hahahahah!

denver history museum. no worries. its fake.

Although we didn't care at the time, I am certainly mortified now that we used to carry around lunchboxes. As purses. In seventh grade. We were quite the trendsetters at the time, and we rapidly grew in numbers. The Lunch Pail Kids. Yes, we even had a name. Eeeeek. I wanted to keep the focus on the lunchbox itself, so I used a large photo and kept the design very simple. I thought the month paper gave the layout a very school house feel, as did the cluster of embellishments.

Kristina Contes

When Ben's mom gave me the sign he made that hung on his old bedroom door, I knew it was perfect for this Dare. I mean seriously: "Beware of dragon"? That's genius. This page is all about the photo and the sign, so I wanted to keep everything else simple. I chose elements that all had some sort of circles (the tape, the background paper, the accent papers) to ensure that everything flowed well and didn't detract from the focus of the layout.

Nisa Fiin

We still wonder how we got the cutest dog ever. Are her tiny outfits not the most precious thing ever? Her person...ality slays me. She is amazing. Our little Egyptian Magician.

CHLOE
Rose

Ribbon

LUCKIEST

Little Hoopty... How did we get so lucky? How did we get the best puppy on Earth? Maybe I should shutup & stop questioning it, And just ENJOY. Love You!

BEING WEIRD ISN'T ENOUGH

HUSBAND & *Wife*

THE SILLY, FUNNY, WACKY

Now that we've trudged through the heavy things in life, let's **lighten it up** a bit. Because **it's fun to scrap**. It doesn't have to be all important events and earth shattering changes. The **silly stuff** is just as much a part of your life as everything else. So **have a little fun** with these Dares.

Dd dog frog cordial
Ff friendly
Cc cherry
Rr rabbit resting
Ss

Aa Bb Cc Dd Ee Ff Gg Hh

before you know it, she'll be singing her ABCs

PERMISSION SLIP:

This Dare is about allowing yourself to do things. Letting yourself be who you want. Letting yourself be free. Allowing yourself to dress like Scuba Steve, put ketchup on your pasta or make up your own words. It's OK. Go ahead, give yourself permission, and create a page about it.

With this Dare I had to ask myself what changes I have seen in me, and the one thing that stood out was that I was finally free of all the negative influences that had burdened me for most of my life. I wanted to place pictures of the things and people that made me happy inside a heart shape and give it wings to portray that my heart was light and free. But as I was working, I wrote a word on each picture and used the picture of my hands as a background on the spur of the moment. My instincts took over while I was working on this page, perhaps because it was so personal.

Michelle Guray

Permission slip is all about allowing yourself to do things. Things you possibly do not want to do, or don't feel you have the right or power to do. I decided to do my page about art. About following my heart. I wanted to give myself permission to do what I love, regardless of whether it's accepted or deemed appropriate. It's OK to do what I love. I am not lazy or flighty if I am an artist.

Kristina Contes

While working on a couple of assignments, I was feeling frustrated. I stopped what I was doing and started just messing around. I made paint splatters and busted out the poster paint pen. I just wanted to make a total mess. Amazingly enough, it evolved into this crazy, fun and totally freeing page. This page accomplished everything I needed at the time and became the perfect permission slip for me.

Genevieve Simmonds

STOP WORRYING.

What, me worry? Only like constantly. I don't know what my deal is. I'm always sweating over something. Sometimes it's specific...sometimes it's just a vague pressing worry. It doesn't actually help anything. Worrying won't "make it better". It doesn't actually FIX anything. Just ties me in knots. I need to let this go. I need to relax. I need to remember: Everything will be ok. In the end. If it's not o.k., it's not the end. Just chill Nisa. It's o.k.

IT IS OK

If there's one thing I seriously need to give myself permission to do it's to stop worrying. Seriously, Nisa. Stop. I used a variety of patterned papers to illustrate how chaotic it is in my head sometimes but laid them out in an orderly fashion to show that despite the chaos, I'm trying to make sense of things in my head. To punch up the distress factor on my main photo, I wet it first and then sanded it.

Nisa Fiin

In this layout, I wanted to remind myself and give myself permission to stay true to me. I wanted to address the fact that I am not living up to my potential, but at the same time, I am doing great things with my life. There are times I am very down on myself, and this page gives me permission to believe in fate, to believe that it all happens for a reason, to be OK with who I am at this moment.

Meghan Heath Dymock

I wanted the focus of this Dare to be on the journaling and to use the journaling as my mission statement. I taped off the edges of the watercolor paper, painted it, let it dry, and added the doodles, journaling and photos.

Sarah Bowen

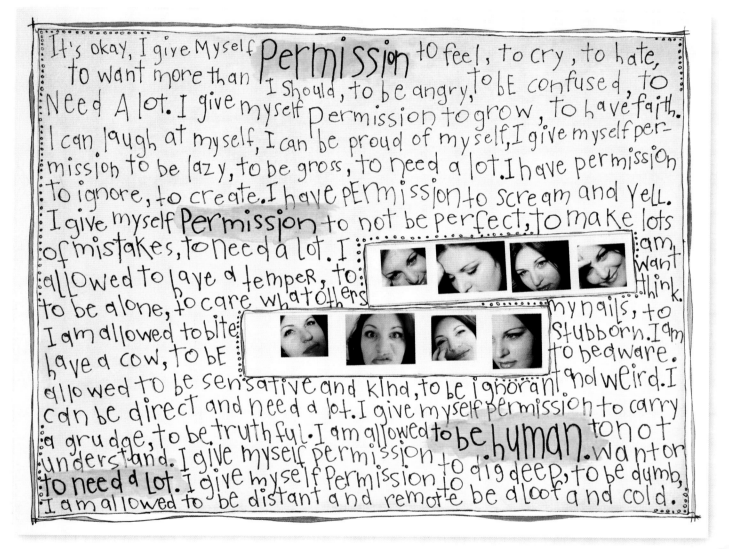

It's okay, I give Myself Permission to feel, to cry, to hate, to want more than I should, to be angry, to be confused, to Need A lot. I give myself Permission to grow, to have faith. I can laugh at myself, I can be proud of myself, I give myself permission to be lazy, to be gross, to need a lot. I have permission to ignore, to create. I have PERMission to scream and Yell. I give myself Permission to not be perfect, to make lots of mistakes, to need a lot. I am allowed to have a temper, to be alone, to care what others want think. I am allowed to bite my nails, to have a cow, to be stubborn. I am allowed to be sensative and kind, to be ignorant. not weird. I can be direct and need a lot. I give myself permission to carry a grudge, to be truthful. I am allowed to be human to not understand. I give myself permission to dig deep, to be dumb. to need a lot. I give myself permission to be aloof and cold. I am allowed to be distant and remote.

SHOES: *We all have 'em. Most of us love 'em. What do your shoes say about you or the people you love? Maybe you hate feet. Maybe you go barefoot and only wear toe rings. Maybe you have 300 pairs of Manolo Blahniks. Whatever. Just get inspired by and create a layout about the ever-so-important topic of footwear.*

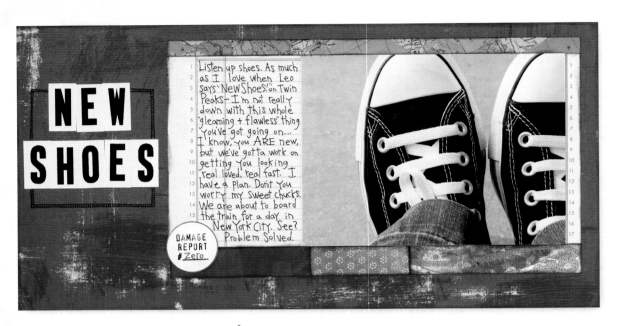

I just had to scrap my chucks. There's nothing better than breaking in a new pair of All Stars. On this layout I used distressed papers to contrast the clean photo of my brand spankin' new shoes and black-and-white letter stickers that balance the black-and-white chucks.

Nisa Fiin

I love my shoes, and I wanted this layout to reflect my free-for-all side. I altered the photos in Photoshop and further altered them with paint and a black pen, letter punches, transparency and tape. The layout just materialized—no rhyme or reason, just fun!

Sarah Bowen

I do love shoes but find my style changing over the years. Let's face it—heels aren't exactly practical for chasing children around. But I still have a fantasy that some day I'll have the reason and motivation to wear some of my hot shoes again. And the cash flow to own even more. But for now my priority is comfort, and I'm totally cool with that.

Genevieve Simmonds

ADD kickin in Hardcore

this phrase was coined a few years ago, in the car with Jonathan & Kreade. I'm all about the continual motion & my footwear can surely attest to that. Total ADD styles. On the go, getting bored, needing new. That's me. Poor shoes take a beating, but they definitely love all the glorious places they've been to for 5.7 seconds.

Since I have fancy shoes and casual shoes, I couldn't decide which ones to scrap. Eventually I realized there was more of a story behind my everyday shoes. I shot all my most worn pairs to convey a feeling of history and all the places they have been. I am very much an "on the go" kind of girl, so I chose to write about how I get bored easily. The story of my friends in the car and how the "ADD kickin' in hardcore" phrase was born was perfect for that photo. I used papers that had a lot of movement in them to go along with the overall theme of action.

Kristina Contes

.fun. .flashy. .fashion able.

worn in the past... now they kill me! i keep thinking maybe one day.....

fantasy

reality.

it's true... i'm pretty much a flip-flops and kicks girl now....

.practical. .boring. .comfy.

LITTLE ME:

Ahh, those good old time-warp photos. The horrific 1970s sofa. The crazy wallpaper. Us in cords with bowl haircuts. For this Dare, scrap a childhood photo of you or someone you know. The older the better. Capture those vintage bits of memorabilia in modern day art.

Here I used one of my all time favorite photos of little me. The layout is about struggling with this whole growing up thing and sometimes wishing I were six. (Funny thing is, after I made this page, I showed it to my mom, who informed me that I hated being six...couldn't wait to grow up. Go figure.) I made my photo transparent by doing a contact paper transfer. I made a color copy of my photo and covered it with contact paper. Then I soaked it in water until the white paper of the color copy was soft enough to rub off, leaving just the image on the contact paper.

Nisa Fiin

PETER
RABBIT
IS
STILL ALIVE!

(incredible!!!)
i remember falling asleep to the
music-box tune he plays. hard to
believe this bunny has survived 29 +
years. he's a little bit more scrungy than
he was back then, and his fur is not quite
as soft. but watching jaxon fall in
love with him over the last little
while has been amazing for me. i'm
really happy that mr. peter rabbit
is still alive and kickin'. september 06

One of my all-time favorite photos of me as
a baby is this one of me clutching my Peter
Rabbit stuffed animal. Just a little while ago,
I discovered Peter Rabbit again and introduced
him to Jaxon. Jaxon took to him right away
and was fascinated with the fact that this little
bunny was mine when I was a baby. I think
having a photo of me with Peter back in 1978
and one of Peter today is pretty cool.

Genevieve Simmonds

My little brother and I grew up together;
we have a shared history. So for me, little me
includes my brother, too. I wanted the focus
to be on us, so I created a monochromatic
background of white paper tiles to add subtle
dimension without distracting from the photo.

Jamaica Edgell

1983.
we look cute and sweet now but for the
next 15 years we were anything but...

we fought.
we kicked & yelled.
we tattled.

we couldn't share
the tv, the couch
or even a bag of cookies.

who knew we'd
emerge from it the
best of friends.

joshua & jaime

Tyson and Brant have been friends since they were seven years old! They always reconnect no matter where they live or what they are doing in their lives. We've always had this photo of them on our refrigerator, and I wanted to showcase it for this Dare. I painted the background paper and then added the photos, frames and stickers. I painted a white box at the bottom of the page to journal on and added their initials.

Meghan Heath Dymock

I am very fortunate to have scanned hundreds of photos from my childhood a few summers ago. This is one of those photos. My family has a long history of owning golden retrievers. This is Kelly, my aunt Debbie's dog, and the first golden that came into my life. I loved her so much, and today I love my golden just as much. I love how happy we both are in this picture.

Laura Kurz

DO NOT

No. ——— Term, 18 ——

Do not, I repeat, not do the perm thing. Your bangs will never be as high as Tiffany's. And not only will you have to live with it as it grows out, it will never fully go away. The bad perm that never dies. Don't do it.

For the little me Dare, I didn't have many options. This is one of the only photos I have from my childhood! It's pretty bad, but oh so funny. The white shirt buttoned all the way to the top is genius. I journaled about the horrible perm I got right before this picture was taken, circa fourth grade. A spiral perm. Sheesh. I wanted to look like Tiffany or Debbie Gibson, but let's face it—I'm doomed to have Marcia Brady hair forever. I used all my favorite supplies on this page to take the focus off my face!

Kristina Contes

I loved scrapping about my childhood. I have a whole series of layouts that start with the phrase, "This little girl...". This one focuses on something my mom told me. She said some of my teachers in my early years told her I was unnatural and didn't act like a child.

Anja Wade

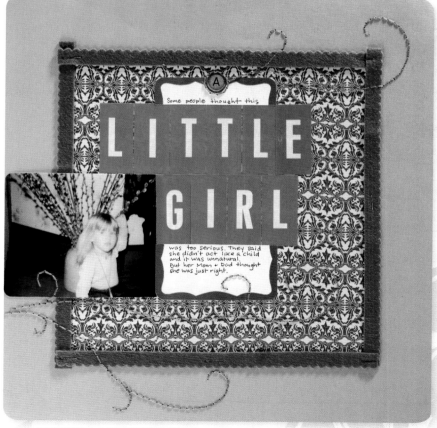

Some people thought this

LITTLE GIRL

was too serious. They said she didn't act like a child and it was unnatural. But her Mom + Dad thought she was just right.

ONE SENTENCE: Describe yourself in one sentence. Chose wisely because you only get one. The best sentences are usually quotes, but any sentence will do. Capture the very essence of you in one singular string of words and put it on a layout.

The idea behind this page is fairly simple—I still have not had that flash of inspiration as to what I want to do with my life. There are so many things I haven't given up on yet (judge, ambassador, rock star). The idea to photograph the journaling came from a challenge to journal on the photos. I don't like my handwriting on slick surfaces so I photographed each word and just adhered them to the layout.

Alison Flynn

I thought about using a quote for this Dare, or trying to figure out exactly what to say in one sentence. One day it dawned on me...I was completely exhausted, done, spent. I wanted to do this one sentence page as therapy. I didn't necessarily think I would use it in the book. But I chose to. Why? Because this was me, exactly how I was and what I was feeling, on that day, in one sentence.

Genevieve Simmonds

This quote was perfect for this Dare. I decided to get a few different photos with different expressions and mix them with black and white as well. The variety lent to a feeling of confusion and whimsy. I repeated the process with my lettering by mixing rub-ons with letter stickers. The use of color and the quote itself are what gives the piece unity.

Kristina Contes

For this Dare I scrapped my fam because, frankly, if I have to narrow all this crazy life down to one sentence, it comes down to them. These people know me inside and out, good and bad—all of it. And I am more than proud to say I am "one of us."

Nisa Fiin

SWAP: *Scrap someone else's pictures. Sometimes the best way to get out of a slump is to try someone else's life on for size. If you have a boy, borrow a kid and scrap some girl pics. If you always scrap your children, scrap yourself. Mix it up. You may find a whole new world just waiting to be discovered.*

I have such an attachment to this child, Jack, who I have never met. I honestly believe that he and my son Jaxon would be soul friends, if only they could meet. This feeling was affirmed by Jack's Aunt Gabby, who felt the same way after having a chance to get to know Jaxon. I e-mailed Jack's mother and asked her to send a photo of him. She sent several, and I couldn't choose, so I used them all. I found the perfect quote and the rest is history.

Genevieve Simmonds

This was a fun Dare. These are Jess Sprague's photos of her little guy. He is just so bright and adorable, so I wanted to use lots of bright colors. I pulled the colors from the photos— specifically his nuks, since that's the focus of the journaling. Scrapping someone else's photos can be a great way to see things in a new way and spark something new in your art.

Nisa Fiin

For this Dare I wanted to create a page about my newest niece, Gracie. This photo was taken when she was four days old. I stood up over my scrapbook table and splashed paint down onto the cardstock. After it dried I added the photo and other elements. Gracie looks so sweet and teeny in this photo. I wanted the page to be feminine and pretty, just like her!

Meghan Heath Dymock

Image Nº

5 tiMeS.

Yup, five. Meg. changed her outfit 5 times on her birthday. She is quite the little fashionista!

I love doing swaps, because they help my mind switch gears and get my creative juices flowing. I've loved Margaret, a daughter of one of Nisa's clients, ever since I saw her photo on Nisa's Web site. I knew immediately that I wanted to scrap pictures of her. I chose three of my favorite photos and wrote about a funny story Nisa told me about her. This girl seems to be my kind of kid. I chose blues and greens to stray away from typical feminine colors; the starburst flowers and rhinestones give the page the girlish charm it deserves without being frilly.

Kristina Contes

caughtonfilm

SEP

Yes. for You small man – when it comes to the NUks – You've gotta have a handful. Two hands full. one NUk in each. A NUk and a spare. At naptime you can even get a little rotation going. This NUk, That NUk, This NUk, That NUk... passes the time before sleep takes over...

ADMIT ONE
two NUks

Baby
gracie
age 4 days

DATE: *We are big fans of numbers around here. Create a layout that features the date as the focal point and title. It could be an important date like an anniversary, or a random one like the day you first ate raw fish. It's quite fun to make a big old number become the main eye catcher.*

I thought a perfect page would be about my sister and her trip to Italy on her own. Aubrie is very independent and booked a trip to Europe, staying in England a few nights by herself before meeting up with a tour group in Italy. Sometimes people will ask me, "Why did she do that?" and I say, "Because she could." She is such an inspiration to me.

Meghan Heath Dymock

I used to hate gin and tonics until the day Tim tricked me into trying one. Now they are my favorite. And ever since that day, he gives me a hard time about "whether this is going to be a G&T thing." So I wanted to remember that day and that I should try new things...before I say I hate them.

Jamaica Edgell

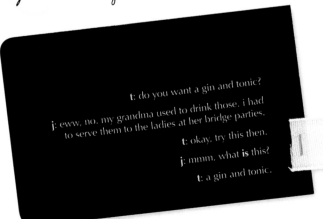

You'll say it's really good to see You.

You'll say I've missed You horribly.

You'll say·let me carry that,
     give that to me.

And You will take the heavy stuff.

And You will drive the car.

And I'll look out the window
     & make jokes about the way things are...

- Ani DiFranco -

2·14·04·

DATE:

For this Dare, I scrapped the first time I drove to Nebraska to visit Ben. About a month after Ben and I starting dating, he moved back to Lincoln for a year of school. This date was a milestone for us: the first time I visited his hometown, the first time I met his family, our first Valentine's Day. And it was the day I realized just how amazing it really was that this boy made this drive every other weekend to see me in Minnesota. This was big.

Nisa Fiin

I absolutely love this series of photos I took at a friend's wedding. I immediately thought of her wedding date for this Dare. I chose colors to frame the photos and keep the focus on them and the title.

Genevieve Simmonds

RIBBON: Who doesn't have tons of ribbon scraps lying around? For this Dare, create a page that rocks the ribbons. Get out your balls of string and create to your heart's content. Make some hang tags, ribbon tabs, bows and frames. Ribbons rule, so get down with the fibers.

We still wonder how we got the cutest dog ever. Are her tiny outfits not the most precious thing ever? Her ... person ... ality slays me. She is amazing. Our little Egyptian Magician.

chloE Rose

HUSBAND & Wife

As one who hoards my favorite products I was very excited to use some of the ribbons from my stash for this Dare. I threw down a strip of double-sided tape and stuck on varying lengths and colors of ribbon. Way too much fun.

Kristina Contes

Inspired by log cabin pillows I'd seen online, I created this page using the same pattern with ribbons and a photo. I selected ribbons to match the wedding colors and made the frame 8" x 10" (20cm x 25cm) so it could be framed in a shadow box. The off-center photo allows room for mementos from the wedding, like dried flowers and a wire chair made from the champagne cork, to be added.

Jamaica Edgell

I've been holding onto this twill for a long time, waiting for just the right use. It's so cute, but a lot of my pages aren't "cute." These photos of Taila were totally perfect.

Genevieve Simmonds

In starting this Dare, I pulled out some of my favorite bright funky ribbons and paired them with a photo of me and my sweet lil' pup— she is just an adorable little firecracker.

Nisa Fiin

THE RANDOM

Why? Because we can. Go ahead and document little **tidbits** of your life that would ordinarily go **unnoticed**. You'll find these are the ones you'll look back at with the most fondness. The **bizarre things** that make your life unique and all your own. Meaningless pieces of an extraordinary life.

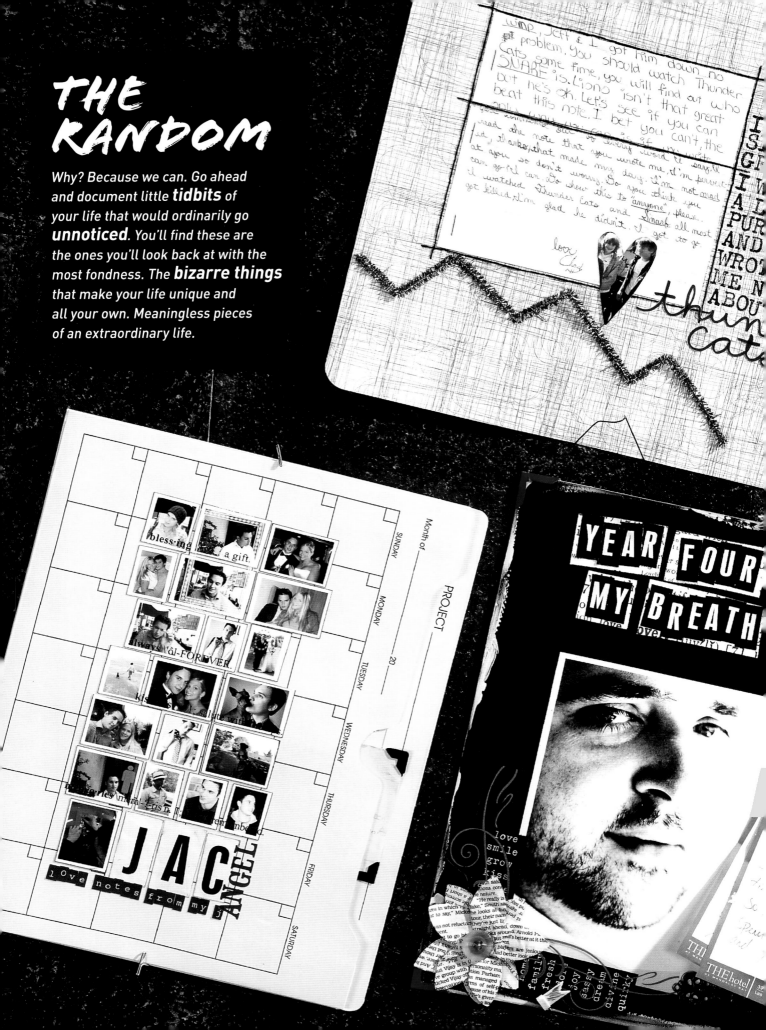

SEVEN RANDOM FACTS: *Your favorite kind of socks. Your child's most overused word. The play he starred in as a fifth grader. Create a page of facts—make them random and make them seven.*

our Random facts

1. I kissed Tyson first... I said "are you gonna kiss me or what?"
2. We carpool to work 3 days a week.
3. Tyson is super chatty in the morning-I'm not!
4. He takes his socks off foot by foot and leaves them in a cute pile on the floor- I love it.
5. I can read a book in a day- a trait I got from my mama.
6. We've been together for seven years.
7. Our favorite thing to do is to snuggle up in bed until we fall asleep then we hold hands most of the night. 12/2006 MHD

7 random facts M & T STYLE

Nisa took this photo of Tyson and me, and I about fell over when I saw it. It is so us. He hates having his photo taken, but she captured him in all his beauty! I love all the randomness we share and wanted this page to reflect our pure love and funny quirks.

Meghan Heath Dymock

this one MOMENT

The cat slept the whole time.

The book is by Xinran

"Venice is sinking" was playing.

The bedspread is from Ikea in Marseille.

There's a stain on my shirt.

It was a very sunny saturday morning.

Ivan had just had a haircut.

AUGUST 2006

I love this series of pictures because it actually looks like us. I just wanted to tell the story behind it—to remember the moment.

Alison Flynn

THIS BOY

Can "rig up" just about anything

Uses super glue instead of band-aids

Has a rad "sing-y face"

Can identify any plane in the sky

Eats my crazy gluten-free food with me

Is beyond hilarious…(though has the world believing he's "quiet")

Has total boy handwriting, but can do wicked awesome calligraphy

B₃

splendid notable   wow   good looking   brilliant   outrageous   divine   so clever

I did this Dare about my Ben. He's pretty quiet around people he doesn't know very well, and I just want everyone to know how flippin' rad and fascinating he is.

Nisa Fiin

one .1 ' ve been meaning to put up curtains in my bedroom for at least 3 years.

two .2 i have a crock pot but have never used it. i want to use it.

3kee 3 i do crazy things to my hair at least twice a year.

four .4 i love yahtzee and boggle and monopoly. and puzzles.

five .5 my cd collection is seriously outdated.

six 6 open cupboard doors make me crazy (see exhibit: pissed off)

seven .7 i love nanaimo bars.

ALL random dom

123456/890

1234567890

This page was so fun—I loved jotting down the first seven tidbits about me that came to mind. I used a picture of me that's a close-up of my red streak after just having my hair "did." I tied that in with a random fact about my wacky hair habits.

Genevieve Simmonds

I focused on things that specifically convey the type of person I am, the things that make me tick. No specific order. Just me in a precise nutshell. I used green as an accent to the overlay because it's my favorite color, so it acts as my eighth random fact without me actually listing it. My own little way of breaking the rules just a little bit.

Kristina Contes

7 random FACTS

REPORT CARD ENCLOSED			
Date	Deliver To	Sent By	Regarding
I can recite all of Ferris Bueller's day off.			1
The Devil wears Prada made me cry.			2
I can't sleep unless I have socks on.			3
I'm on a Dashboard Confessional CD.			4
If it's camo, I will buy it.			5
I think way too much.			6
I have 5 tattoos & 6 piercings.			7

Please Acknowledge Receipt

4115260000

7

one	YOU LOVE GETTING THINGS IN THE MAIL.
two	BEFORE YOU GO TO SLEEP, YOU ALWAYS NEED YOUR BACK SCRATCHED.
three	TOYS, TOYS, TOYS! THEY'RE ALWAYS ON YOUR MIND.
four	YOU THINK THE BEST WAY TO TAKE A BATH IS WITH LOTS AND LOTS OF BUBBLES.
five	YOU ONCE SAID, "THE BEST PART ABOUT SCHOOL IS RECESS!"
six	EATING IS VERY HARD FOR YOU.
seven	YOU LIKE DOING CRAFTS WITH MOMMY AND PLAYING VIDEO GAMES WITH DADDY.

SEP 2006

Listing seven random facts about my son was easy. In fact, I could have listed more, but I chose the ones that were most noticeable. I think my green, yellow and black color scheme is very boyish. Also, dandelions were his "thing" when he was younger, so I loved incorporating the image onto this page. This photo of my son isn't posed; he was totally into playing with his toy. It was him doing one of the things he loves best.

Michelle Guray

I think the simple, mundane things that happen every day in our lives will be the most fascinating to look back on fifty years from now. I chose to record seven random facts about one regular day. No pictures, just words.

Jill Hornby

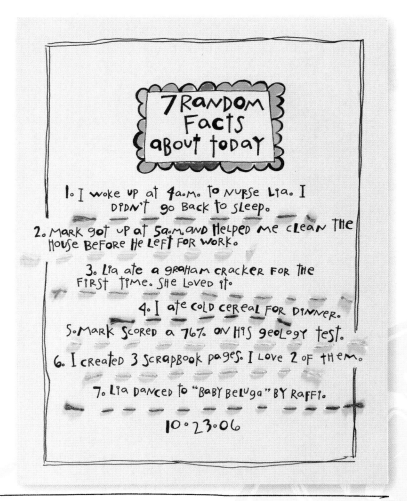

7 RANDOM FACTS ABOUT TODAY

1. I woke up at 4 a.m. to nurse Lia. I didn't go back to sleep.
2. Mark got up at 5 a.m. and helped me clean the house before he left for work.
3. Lia ate a graham cracker for the first time. She loved it.
4. I ate cold cereal for dinner.
5. Mark scored a 76% on his geology test.
6. I created 3 scrapbook pages. I love 2 of them.
7. Lia danced to "Baby Beluga" by Raffi.

10·23·06

FOUND OBJECT: The beauty of scrapping is that there are so many materials laying around just waiting to be used on a page. Go digging through your junk drawers, flip through some magazines, and create a page using a "non" scrap supply. We find that wrapping paper, office supplies and clothing tags are easily accessible and especially fun.

I loved this title and arrow that I found in a magazine.

Jamie Bagley

This quote, from a wedding favor, was a total inspiration for this page. Paired with the photos, I realized this page was my fairy tale. I used photos Jaxon took on Daddy's bus...total fun.

Genevieve Simmonds

I throw away so many of these wallet photo leftovers in my photo business, but one day I looked at them and realized that some of them were really colorful and funky. I thought it would be great to divide a layout into little vignettes. It was fun to scrap this bit of throw-away stuff and make it work as art.

Nisa Fiin

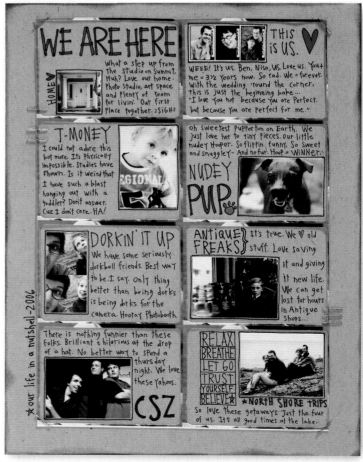

Do You ReMember That dAy? It WAS tHe DAY We rOde daDDYs BUS ANd yOU TOOk PicTuRes and even tHouGh it miGHt NOT seem Like your aveRAGe faRY tALe Well ITs MY FaRY TALe Ok?! Ok

ok

ok

"ONCE IN A WHILE, RIGHT IN THE MIDDLE OF AN ORDINARY LIFE, LOVE GIVES US A FAIRY TALE ..."

OuR story TOGETHER

dk

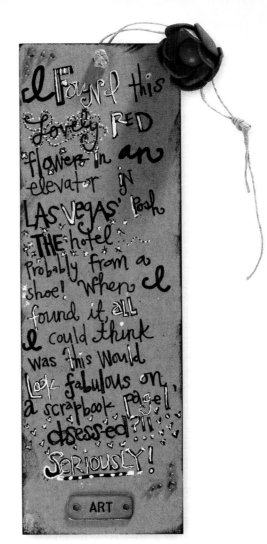

I Found this Lovely RED flower in an elevator in LAS Vegas Posh THE hotel Probably from a shoe! When I found it, all I could think was this Would Look fabulous on a scrapbook page! obsessed?!!! SeriOUSLY!

ART

I couldn't believe my luck when I found this red flower in a Las Vegas elevator! I knew instantly I would use it for this Dare. I wanted to be able to see this cute red flower every day, so I made it into a sign to hang in my studio that talks about my obsession with art supplies. Every time I see it, I am reminded of that trip to Las Vegas and how completely happy I am to have art in my life.

Meghan Heath Dymock

LIFE is not MEASURED by the NUMBER of BREATHS we take the NUMBER of MOMENTS that our BREATH AWAY

I've had this clay pot from Williams-Sonoma for a while, and this Dare was the perfect time for me to finally use it. I decided to make a circular mini accordion album about our family in 2006 to go inside. I used a bunch of different ribbons to attach each page, and then used those ribbons as my color base to create all the pages. I love looking at this album because it captures so many different fun memories from that year.

Kristina Contes

FIERCE: One word. What does fierce mean to you?
What do you think of? The possibilities are endless. Scrap it.

fierce

This woman is fierce. She may not believe it now, but it's true. She will start her own business. She will have three amazing kids,... For much of their lives, she will be a single mom. She will be a phenomenal mom. She will have some seriously hard times and not let on to her kids at all. They will be loved so hugely and will be blissfully unaware of a lot of her sacrifices until they are adults. She will endure heartbreak and stress and worries and she will come out on top. Fam in tow. Holding our hands while we all safely cross the next street, the next hurdle, the next bump in the road. She will be an inspiration. She will be an unending support... She just doesn't know it yet.

There was no doubt that my fierce Dare had to be about my mom. She is phenomenal—so strong and brilliant and seriously fierce. I pulled colors from her sweet shirt for my layout. Luckily they were strong, complementary colors and really worked. Love when that happens.

Nisa Fiin

"Fierce" is many things to me, but it's definitely going nuts in public when having fun with friends. I love the memories I've made acting like a total goofball, ending up in fits of laughter at the end. This photo of Kristi reminded me of that feeling, and I immediately came up with the idea of using fabric to make buildings and sewing all over the place.

Genevieve Simmonds

The first thing that comes to mind when I think of the word fierce? New York City. So I scrapped it. I used a few different random photos that capture the city from my perspective. I used corrugated cardboard to give it a gritty, industrial look and a quote from the Beastie Boys that sums it up perfectly. My love for Manhattan surely deserves a spot in my scrapbooks!

Kristina Contes

I created this page after I had a miscarriage. I wanted it to be shocking and frightening and sad all at the same time. Every time I look at it, I am reminded of what we went through with our first pregnancy; the fear, heartbreak and anger are all on this page. The clock signifies time, and the M with the wings signifies that I am a strong woman who will survive this.

Meghan Heath Dymock

THINGS I DO: *Random bits about our lives that we want to capture.*

Here's an excuse to scrap the little things that no one else would really understand, like your husband's bumper stickers or the way you place things on your windowsill above the sink. When someone else flips through your scrapbook, they will see this page and squeal, "You totally do that!" or "That's so you!" or "I do that too!" and before you know it you have a new best friend.

Sunday-night sushi became a bit of a habit when Dren was working the evening shift. He would be starving afterward and would bring home sushi to share. Not only did the sushi totally rock, but it was nice to spend a little time together before I went to bed. I'm a little glad we have broken the habit (for now), but only because I'm sure it's not the best plan to eat right before bed!

Genevieve Simmonds

This Dare began as a series of pages I made to document all the quirky "unscrapable" things I wanted to remember. One thing I do quite frequently is recite Beastie Boys lyrics. I love them. They are one of my favorite bands of all time, and I constantly rock my "No Sleep Til" shirt. So clearly I sweat the Beasties. I used an old CD and some camouflage tape to convey a street vibe. What a great thing to pay homage to on this page.

Kristina Contes

Observation

WHEN WE'RE APART I TRY TO FIND WAYS TO MAKE OTHER PEOPLE SAY YOUR NAME

Things I do...

RESULTS

DISCUSSION

EVIDENCE

I saw this quote a few years ago, and it's just perfect for this Dare. I am just so smitten with this boy, it's not even funny. Even hearing his name makes my insides happy.

Nisa Fiin

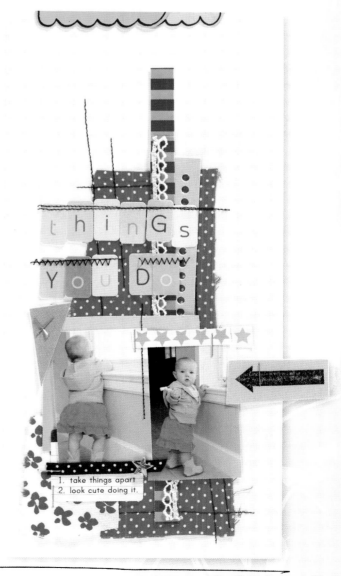

I didn't have anything profound to say here. I just wanted to have fun. I layered fabric, paper and ribbon and sewed it all together. I tried to use lots of fun colors without making them clash with the photo.

Jill Hornby

NOTE: *Scrap a note from someone or one you've written. Notes from your husband, something you put in your child's lunchbox, a note from a friend...these are invaluable and deserve a home in your scrapbook pages! Don't pretend you don't have any, because as scrapbookers, it's in our genetic code to save these sorts of things.*

You wrote this one time when we were out eating hoagies and soup at Acoustic Cafe years ago... sometime in those "college-y" years. We talked and laughed and scribbled down a ton that night in the notebook I brought along...but this note I saved. "A husband & children & swing sets made of wood, real soon. I promise!" I remember thinking how perfect and dreamy and far-off it seemed. And yet how much I wanted it even then. For both of us. I loved this. So I saved it. I have moved how many flippin' times since then? Like seven or something ridiculous. I'm sure countless semi-precious things have been lost, left behind in each packing up of my life. But this has survived. I hung on to this...as if you writing it and me saving it would make it so...

We are closer than ever my dear...

a Husband & children & swingsets made of wood... real soon. I promise!

I dug out this note by my friend Sarah from its safe place, where it has lived through several moves. I am a saver of these kinds of things; love me a good note. But this has to be one of my favorites. So simple, but it's so real and somehow says so much.

Nisa Fiin

ee e esdfgh;klyam1w6 s

        jytreeedfe'h kl:4qwe rtyu 1o ;-=zxc rbm nm, /¢
13243456788 90-=

LOVE LETTER

u ubu u u   72   7 7 77 7   ; 7 7 7

It says, "Love you."

My son was playing on my typewriter and gave me this paper. He said he had a letter for me, and that it said "Love you." So good.

Linda Buranasakorn

For this Dare, I knew I wanted to use notes from Jonathan. I have so many I decided to use a folder that could house them all. I treasure every single note, even if it just says to take out the garbage. Anytime I see his handwriting, I smile. Especially if he draws something—those are the best.

Kristina Contes

YEAR FOUR AND I LOSE MY BREATH EACH TIME

For this Dare, I decided to scrapbook the note my husband wrote me on our fourth wedding anniversary. I took this photo of Tyson on that anniversary while we were staying in Las Vegas. He is so handsome; he still takes my breath away with his good looks and his kindness.

Meghan Heath Dymock

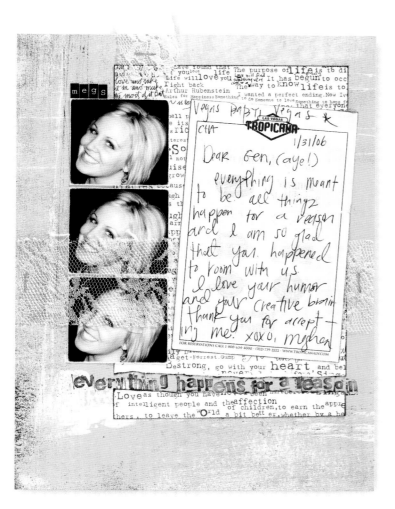

I received this note from Meg a few months before I joined the group. I was touched that she wrote the note and was glad to learn I affected her in a positive way. I held onto it and was so happy to have the chance to use it on a page. Of course, it would have to feature the gorgeous Meg herself—times three. This was an awesome page to do for *this* book.

Genevieve Simmonds

This Dare made me immediately think of some notes I still have tucked away that were written by my sixth grade boyfriend. They make me smile. I made the sparkly pipe cleaner into the shape of lightning.

Anja Wade

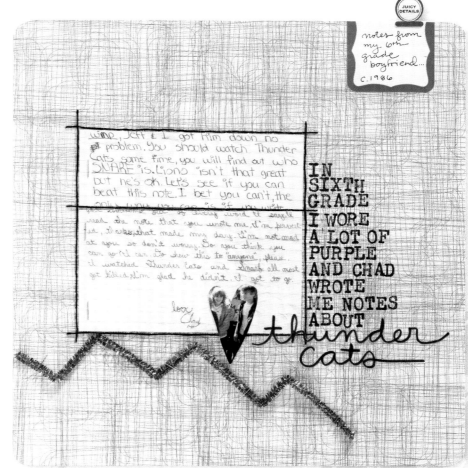

UNIFORM: *What do you wear every day? Clothes so often define who we are. What defines your image? Sweatpants and socks? Do you deplore the idea of being labeled? Or do you revel in the fact that you get to wear kick-ass business suits? Explore your image and what it says to others. Scrap your uniform.*

There was no doubt what I would scrap for the uniform Dare—I live in hoodies. Every day. Winter, spring, summer and fall. I am decked out in hoodies, whatever the weather. They are so cozy, so broken in, so much a part of me.

Nisa Fiin

My uniform has been so incredibly random over the years, but two staples have been a big fat bun full of hair on top of my head and some hoops. To celebrate these uniform items, I chose a photo that included both. Otherwise the layout is simple, with patterned paper to add just a flash of color and raw chipboard letters that spell the phrase that says it all.

Genevieve Simmonds

Since most days I'm either at our restaurant or home creating art, I get to dress however I want. I decided to use a bunch of detail shots of things I wear every day. I loved the report card, and the color palette just flowed from there.

Kristina Contes

This page came about after realizing I had so many pictures of Jake in the same "outfit." He was a nature boy through and through for a few years actually, and I thought it would be a funny reminder years down the road.

Erica Hernandez

INSPIRATION EVERYWHERE: *Anything that inspires you.*

As artists, we tend to make mental notes of pretty much everything. The window at Anthroplogie, a cool movie poster, magazine ads, music videos, books—the list goes on for miles. Find a favorite inspiration piece and make a page using the design or concept.

The one thing that always gets me going and makes me truly think about my art is Bruce Mau's *An Incomplete Manifesto for Growth*. I have it saved in my bookmarks and read it all the time. I decided that would be the perfect thing to use for this Dare. There are 43 growth steps that I wanted to document, but that's a lot of pages for a mini book. So I used string and button envelopes as pages and created little tags to tuck inside. I used a wide range of colors and textures to illustrate the different ideas, pretty much anything I loved or found inspiring.

Kristina Contes

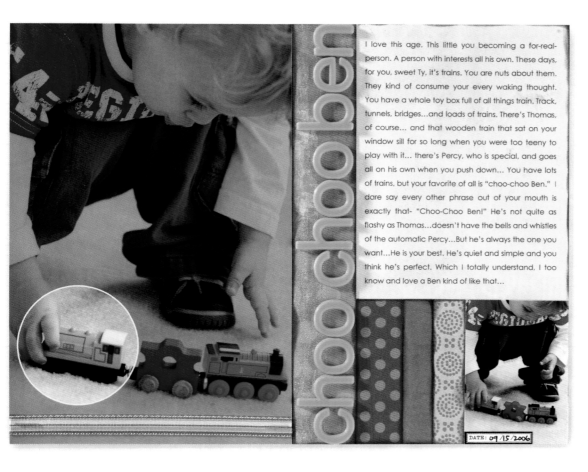

I love this age. This little you becoming a for-real-person. A person with interests all his own. These days, for you, sweet Ty, it's trains. You are nuts about them. They kind of consume your every waking thought. You have a whole toy box full of all things train. Track, tunnels, bridges...and loads of trains. There's Thomas, of course... and that wooden train that sat on your window sill for so long when you were too teeny to play with it... there's Percy, who is special, and goes all on his own when you push down... You have lots of trains, but your favorite of all is "choo-choo Ben." I dare say every other phrase out of your mouth is exactly that- "Choo-Choo Ben!" He's not quite as flashy as Thomas...doesn't have the bells and whistles of the automatic Percy...But he's always the one you want...He is your best. He's quiet and simple and you think he's perfect. Which I totally understand. I too know and love a Ben kind of like that...

DATE: 09/15/2006

choo choo ben

My friend Jess does this great blog that shows a new Photoshop technique every Friday. It's so great! She is so inspiring with all her tutorials. This one, about how to feature a selection of your photo, really caught my eye and inspired me to use it on a layout.

Nisa Fiin

I found inspiration from the Dave Matthews Band song "Steady As We Go" because Tyson is so steady, and we are steady together even in the middle of chaos. I wanted to make this page to show him that he is my favorite person and that I look to him to steady me whenever I am a mess! I brushed paint on the background and lightly foam stamped the background. I used two photos because look at his gorgeous eyes!

Meghan Heath Dymock

steady as we go

you keep me steady as we go ....

when the storm comes down you shelter me when I don't say a word and you know exactly what I mean in the darkest times, you shine on me.

Why I Scrap

this is what **Scrapbooking** means to me...

I remember about a year + 1/2 ago... talking with Ben... about my sad lack of friends. All the people who had moved away, or grown apart. I was feeling a lil' lost and alone. 'Course I had Ben & Hoopty, but where were my girls at?* Then magically, perfectly-along came Scrapbooking * Scrapbooking swooped in and took over. It is my art, my love, my life. It is about remembering, recording, making a mess, creating and telling my story.* But in addition to all that it is about connecting.* I have met some of the most amazing people through this art. I have forged seriously HUGE friendships. online and in real life... across the country and the next city over. We hangout, we scrap, we talk on the phone everyday, email nonstop. For me this is what it's all about... sharing my art and my mess and my passion with these amazing women. LOVE!!

THE POINT

i SCRAP.

Use Other Side

...cheesy, right? this is why...

...better life. it is... ...therapy, the ART... ...the accomplishments... ...realizing the import-... ...this year... and I... ...thankful for... ...her, more patient... ...adds to my life... ...friends to my... ...have met ok... ...me think about... ...done my life withou-...

cat's pajamas

reez

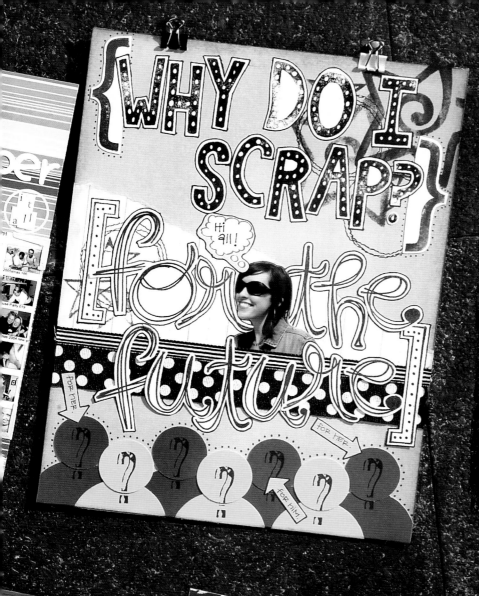

THE BEST

The **very reason** most of us started scrapping in the first place. Those **amazing moments** and **wonderful stories** that are just straight up **epic**. Pages you want to create, blow up to poster size and hang above your fireplace. The **very best** things that you want to **shout from the rooftops**.

BEING A WOMAN:

The virtues of femininity. Being soft and vulnerable and strong all at the same time. Since most scrappers are female (sorry boys!), we dedicate this Dare to you. Create a page that celebrates womanhood and all the things that go along with the estrogen.

I definitely wanted to use a pretty book for this Dare. I found this box at work and knew it would make a perfect home for a mini book. It makes me so happy and inspired when I come across random elements that are perfect for making art and scrapbooking. Paired with photos of stuff I loved, all the goodness was just screaming to come together.

Genevieve Simmonds

I'm drawn to girly things, so I made that the focus of this layout. Girly patterned paper, rhinestones and glitter all add to the look.

Anja Wade

For this Dare, I decided to document all the quirky things only women can do. I threw in some sentimental things as well just for good measure. I chose pink, of course, and added a female sign and the stamped faces to give it a girly vibe. I was very excited to use my vintage pink ribbon and measuring tape to tie into the feminine theme. I made the stamped images a little gritty with distress embossing powder to contrast the softness of the fringe and to further demonstrate the complexity of a woman.

Kristina Contes

THE LITTLE THINGS: Tiny things that make huge differences in your life. A seemingly ordinary routine that actually expresses so much more. Scrap about the little things that have a big impact.

This quote perfectly expresses how parents feel when their kids are happy or sad. It's such a small thing—your child just being happy. And you really don't know how true this quote is until you have a child, that when they're happy, it makes you happy.

Linda Buranasakorn

Tyson hates to have his photo taken. When I saw this photo of him looking at me with so much love in his eyes, I cried a little. That little look is so beautiful to me! I never want him to stop seeing me this way, and I knew I had to create a page so I will always remember how much love he has for me, even if he hates to have his photo taken.

Meghan Heath Dymock

I Crack You Up

loopy   wacky   life is too important to be taken seriously —oscar wilde

OCT 3 0 2006

I suppose it's no huge deal... just a little thing really... But it makes my heart happy. I can make you laugh like it's my damn job (actually it kind of used to be. HA!) I just know what it takes

to get you crackin' up. It's just a little thing. but let me tell you- When I've been having a bad day- Little you laughing is gigantic! ★

While hanging out with my lil' pal Ty the other day, listening to his giggle, I realized that that sound—just his little gigglicious self going crazy over something I said—made everything else, all those big life things, go away. Somehow, this little thing, me cracking him up, is also a really, really big thing.

Nisa Fiin

I was saving this photo for a day when I really wanted to scrapbook just for fun. Laughing is truly one of the smallest things that can make you feel so good. Dren and I are constantly goofing around, doing and saying things to make each other howl. The smallest things deserve to be celebrated.

Genevieve Simmonds

and forever make wish that we can share these moments and feel these feelings a whole lotta fun.- november '06

i would like to always !

ARMY

123456

TRIBUTE PAGE: *A dedication of sorts. This Dare is all about paying homage to the greats. Family members, friends and heroes. Scrap about them— this is your chance to show them all that they mean to you.*

it's been such a treat getting to know you BetteR. we love having you around. XOXOXO

This Dare was a no-brainer for me. I absolutely adore my mother. I feel very lucky to have the kind of mother that I can hang out with, go to for advice, laugh with and cry with. And I'm so happy that she's "retired" with a more flexible schedule, so we can see each other more and I can get to know her even better.

Genevieve Simmonds

Oh yes. this is my Jonathan. the man I married a year and a half ago. Oh so handsome and oh so sweet. But things definately get a little crazy when you become "one." some days he is the most adorable, caring and tidy man. Other days he can be the biggest slob I've ever seen (sorry babe.) But that is what marriage is all about. Identifying & filling in the holes as the personalities mesh. I think there is beauty in the differences. He's a little messy, I'm completely anal. He's so Kind & polite, I am totally Rough. But we even eachother out. Even though we aren't exactly perfect, we complete eachother like

so handsome

a puzzle. what more could we ask for? I've found someone who "gets" me. And I "get" him. so amazing to me. And so handsome!

For the tribute Dare I naturally wanted to do a page about my husband. Since I wanted to keep the focus on the journaling, I kept it simple and just made one of my mosaic frames to go around his photo. The journaling is very honest and real— a perfect tribute to the man of my dreams.

Kristina Contes

I've been wearing Gram's ring...it's still bent to the shape of her finger

I take it off to look at that all the time...makes me feel close to her

I wanted my page to be a tribute to my grandmother. I wish I had more photos of us together or of her when she was young. Instead I have the ring she wore every day. I can see it on her hand in my mind's eye. Now I wear it every day, and when I look down at it on my hand, I remember her. So the ring is front and center. The wood grain paper adds a vintage feel, while the bright green grass and purple paper add some color.

Jamaica Edgell

tribute:TO US

for making the hard decision...for taking a risk...for selling our house, leaving our jobs and moving two babies over 2400 miles. Still struggling are nowhere insurance, no retirement to rely happy and more importantly, our boys are thriving. I'm proud of us for making sacrifices for the good of our family and confident that someday, it will all pay off.

I won't lie—we're financially, we have stable. No savings, no retirement. But, we are

Chinese dinner of fortune 2.28.01
A GREAT DAY LIES AHEAD IN THE NOT TOO DISTANT FUTURE
PANDA EXPRESS • PANDA INN
move date 3.02.01

The decision to move was really a monumental one for our family. We left a house and a reliable income to move thousands of miles away to no house and no job because we felt it would be best for our family in the long run. It was a huge risk, and we've struggled now for a couple of years to right ourselves. But we're almost there, and I'm proud of us for making the tough choice. It's important for our kids to recognize and appreciate the sacrifice that brought us here.

Erica Hernandez

This Dare was really therapeutic for me. This page is about my aunt, who I adored, and who died of cancer just over ten years ago. The words here are adapted from a song that's actually about a break-up...but a loss is a loss. This photo is from a family trip we took to the zoo. We all had a blast. We knew she was sick, but I don't think any of us realized how sick she really was. This was the last outing we all had together.

Nisa Fiin

if someone said 3 months from now you'd be long gone

i'd stand up and punch them out.

miss you forever.

For this Dare, I chose to do a layout about my siblings, my four brothers and two sisters-in-law, and how they add so much joy to my life. I used a paper piercer to poke holes along my pencil sketches, then stitched the design with embroidery floss.

Anja Wade

My sister is my best friend, and I wanted to showcase our relationship for this Dare. I love every minute I get to spend with her, even though I hated her when she was born. I was the only child for four years, and it was quite a transition for me. I especially love the large photo of us because it shows the bond we have now.

Meghan Heath Dymock

WHY I SCRAP:
We all started for a reason. Be it the birth of a child, a wedding, or just some cool girl on the Internet, something got you hooked on this crazy art form. For this Dare, document the reason you still scrapbook. We know there are plenty, so focus on one, or create a layout showcasing the plethora of reasons you can't stop scrapping.

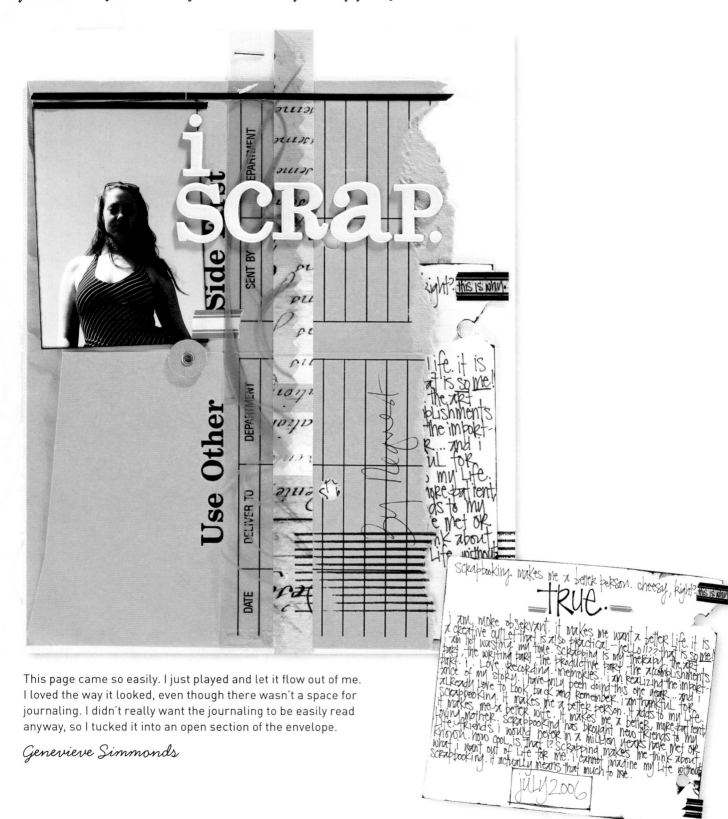

This page came so easily. I just played and let it flow out of me. I loved the way it looked, even though there wasn't a space for journaling. I didn't really want the journaling to be easily read anyway, so I tucked it into an open section of the envelope.

Genevieve Simmonds

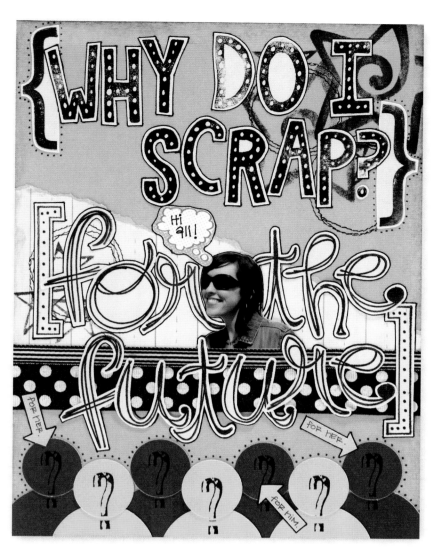

I scrap for the future, so I made "future" people at the bottom of my page.

Jamie Bagley

For this Dare, I knew immediately my page would be about my grandmother and her loss of memory. The page started with the journaling, my story that couldn't have been written with the same feeling by anyone other than me. And that is exactly what scrapbooking is to me, as well as what I say in my last line of journaling: Nobody can record my stories but me.

Jessica Fulkerson

why

I found this picture of my Grandma Lillie holding a camera and my heart stopped. Did I get my love of photography from her? Did she document her life like me? I looked through the suitcase of black and white pictures she left behind and realized that we may never know the stories attached to them...

It's been years since she got Alzheimer's and one year since she passed away and I am still filled with anger that her stories are gone. I was too young to understand their importance and how amazing they could be. And then they were stolen from her and then her stolen from us.

I want to hear about her fears as a young woman, her struggles in marriage, her feelings about becoming a mother, her dreams, her life lessons.

But it's too late.

GONE

don't forget

So I record my own stories. For myself. For my family. For someone who may want to hear them when I can no longer tell them myself. Because nobody can tell my stories but me.

this is what
Scrapbooking
means to me...

I remember...
about a year + ½
ago...talking with Ben...
about my sad lack of
friends. All the people who
had moved away, or grown
apart... I was feeling a lil lost and
alone. Course I had Ben & Hoopty,
but where were my girls at?★ Then
magically, perfectly-along came Scrapbooking ★ Scrapbooking swooped in and
took over. It is my art, my love, my life.
It is about remembering, recording, making
a mess, creating art, telling my story. ★
But in addition to all that, it is about
connecting. ★ I have met some of the
most amazing people through this art. I
have forged seriously HUGE friendships,
online and in real life... across the
country and the next city over. We
hangout, we scrap, we talk on the phone
everyday, email nonstop. For me this is
what it's all about... sharing my art
and my mess and my passion with
these amazing ladies. LOVE♥

IMPORTANT

cat's pajamas

try
to
freeze time
try to freeze time for your mind,
perfect snapshot to always rewind
3|11

Scrappin'...it's my art, my outlet. It helps me
remember and make sense of my life. I scrap
for so many reasons, but one of the best parts
really is all the amazing artists I have met.
People who love this scrapping thing; people
who get it. On this layout I used a ton of little
photos to show the people I have met through
this crazy art/hobby/scrappin' thing. There is
just something so incredible about meeting
and connecting with people who are as
passionate about this art as I am. So amazing.

Nisa Fiin

The reason I scrap is to capture moments.
Pieces of our lives that may otherwise be
forgotten are now immortalized by my
art. The quote by 311 is the perfect way to
explain why I scrap.

Kristina Contes

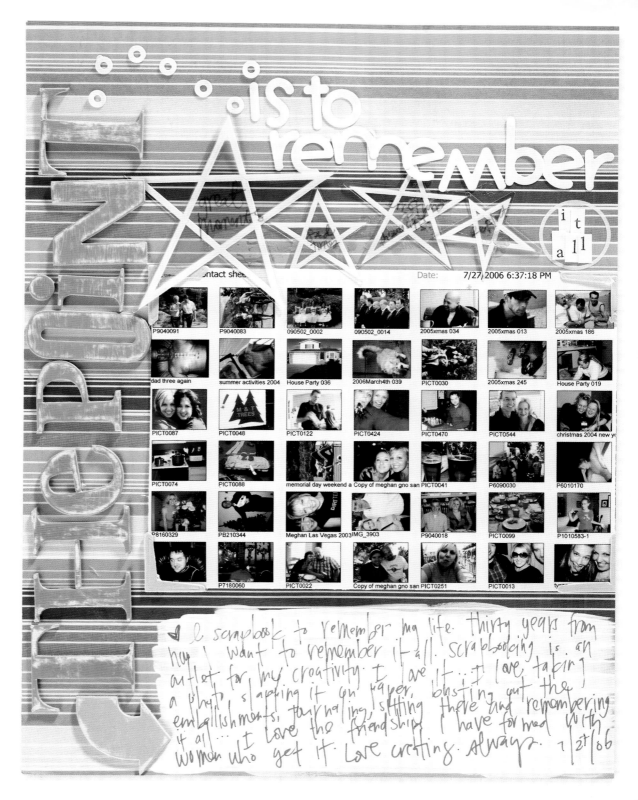

The point is to remember it all

is to remember

Every time I make a scrapbook page, I think about how future generations will view it. I really try to catch the emotion, humor, and life in every one of them because I hope to God that some day someone will want to know what I was like at this age. What I looked like, what I cared about, what I thought was funny, and who I loved. If my ancestors had done something like this I would have pored over those books like it was my job. In my eyes, that's why it's so important to scrapbook.

Meghan Heath Dymock

FRIENDS: *Where would we be without them? Friends make life so much more colorful. Sometimes as scrappers we focus so much on our families, so for this Dare, create a page that gives a shout out to your buddies.*

why can't we be **friends**

♥Sweet lil Hooper, I know you are smitten with the birdies, But somehow I don't think they feel the same.

these girls

So, this isn't the typical "friends" layout. Every time we go to my mom's house, Hooper "discovers" these birds, like she's never seen them before. It just cracks me up how she looks at these birds. She could not be happier to have met them, but she just doesn't understand that they don't so much feel the same way.

Nisa Fiin

Since these girls are such an important part of my life right now, I chose to make a collage of all the different photos we've taken together. I used my stickers as my journaling because I thought they really explained what our relationship is all about. Strength and bonding and support. I used four ribbons down the left side to represent the four of us and used mirrors for their initials to contrast the grittiness of the title.

Kristina Contes

This picture always strikes a good chord in me. It was taken shortly after we first met. Here we are sitting, smiling and having an awesome time on a gorgeous summer day. I love it because we were right in the beginning stages of our friendship, not knowing how close we would become or how quickly. Now we are so close, and have 8 million pictures of the two of us. This one's more special than the rest though because it was one of the first. I cherish it.

Jamie Bagley

There's been some stuff going on in my life lately and my amazing friend Tanya is being such a wonderful help. The concept was to write a letter to her but still treat it like a scrapbook page. To make the envelope more detailed and interesting, I chopped a section out and added a transparency. Dressing up standard office products is totally easy and fun.

Genevieve Simmonds

COLLECTIONS: *Your treasures. Your precious little bitties. Most people have some sort of collection. Scrap yours. The more bizarre the better.*

I don't collect much, and generally don't like knicknacks. They take up room and must be dusted. But I remembered my dad's old Olympic pin collection, and how after 20 years he still treasures it. Collections may take up room and clutter the place, but if it makes you happy, then it might be worth something after all.

Linda Buranasakorn

This page is somewhat of a confession because I've never told anyone that I get a little annoyed if they have more art supplies than I have! Now everyone will know! I love adding elements to pages that never seem like they would work together until I start adding them and they look funky and a little messy. For this page, I wanted to add as many embellishments as I could to reflect all the supplies I own. I love buying scrapbook supplies almost as much as I love using them!

Meghan Heath Dymock

Although I have many collections, my scents are one of my favorites. I used pretty floral paper and a flowing font to convey a sense of luxury. The velvet paper and bird tie into the theme of femininity. To keep it from getting too soft, I used a chartreuse accent and brown lettering. I journaled about the scents and how they hold so much memory. I love how fragrance plays such a huge role in mood and identity.

Kristina Contes

Jaxon definitely loves to collect things, but he's always had this cool fascination with rocks. I must have passed that on to him during trips to the beach when he was just a wee thing. My mum loves to sift through rocks at the beach, too. I'm glad Jaxon can enjoy it with both of us. We set up some of his collection with dinosaur skeleton models, and now he even adds to it when he comes across a nice rock in the city.

Genevieve Simmonds

HOME: *Eventually, it all leads back to home. It could be a physical place. A feeling. A period in time. A person. What does home mean to you? You can scrap pictures of your house, or a person's face. Whatever home means to you, create a page about it.*

I am one who has never really had a real home. I've moved around a lot and never really felt settled in my life. So to me, home is with my family, and my family is Jonathan and Chloe. I used a cluster of photos to show that no matter where we are, as long as I'm with them I feel safe and at home. I used a warm yellow because it felt cozy. The patterned paper says "Celebrate the Everyday," which I thought went perfectly with the theme. I painted the stickers to match the background cardstock and to give it a bit more contrast.

Kristina Contes

For this Dare, I decided to scrapbook my family: The Heath Five. I worked with many old photos and a few new ones to create a massive collage with hidden number fives throughout the layout. I journaled around the layout with the labels and made sure to have a photo with Tyson and me in it with the "5 to 6" label because he has officially created The Heath Six!

Meghan Heath Dymock

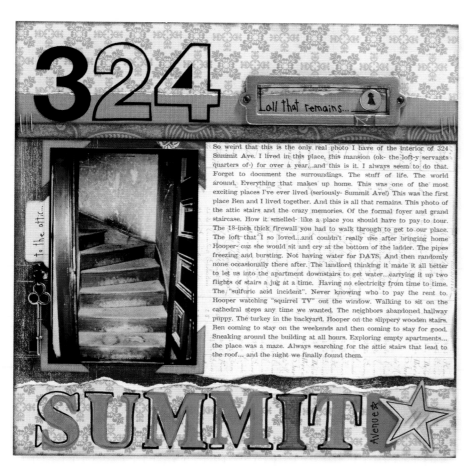

324

all that remains...

So weird that this is the only real photo I have of the interior of 324 Summit Ave. I lived in this place, this mansion (ok- the loft-y servants quarters of-) for over a year...and this is it. I always seem to do that. Forget to document the surroundings. The stuff of life. The world around. Everything that makes up home. This was one of the most exciting places I've ever lived (seriously- Summit Ave!) This was the first place Ben and I lived together. And this is all that remains. This photo of the attic stairs and the crazy memories. Of the formal foyer and grand staircase. How it smelled- like a place you should have to pay to tour. The 18-inch thick firewall you had to walk through to get to our place. The loft that I so loved...and couldn't really use after bringing home Hooper- cuz she would sit and cry at the bottom of the ladder. The pipes freezing and bursting. Not having water for DAYS. And then randomly none occasionally there after. The landlord thinking it made it all better to let us into the apartment downstairs to get water...carrying it up two flights of stairs a jug at a time. Having no electricity from time to time. The "sulfuric acid incident". Never knowing who to pay the rent to. Hooper watching "squirrel TV" out the window. Walking to sit on the cathedral steps any time we wanted. The neighbors abandoned hallway puppy. The turkey in the backyard. Hooper on the slippery wooden stairs. Ben coming to stay on the weekends and then coming to stay for good. Sneaking around the building at all hours. Exploring empty apartments... the place was a maze. Always searching for the attic stairs that lead to the roof... and the night we finally found them.

to the attic...

SUMMIT Avenue ☆

This layout is about the place I lived when Ben and I met. So, first it was my place, but it grew to be our place—our first place. It was an amazing place; we lived in a loft on the third floor of an old mansion on Summit Avenue. There was always something crazy going on in that building. Lots of ups and downs, always an adventure. I loved the place, and it's so crazy that the only real photo I have of it is this one of the stairs to the attic. It makes me realize I should appreciate wherever "home" is while we're there.

Nisa Fiin

I don't have a specific, set place I call home. Since I left for college at 17, I haven't planted my roots in one single place. Moving to a new house every several months... Growing, changing... So for me, "home" is many places, many feelings, many things.

ⓐ

ⓑ **I feel home :**

- whenever I sink my toes into a sandy beach
- when I see my parents kiss each other
- as I crawl into Scott's arms at night
- behind the walls I've built up emotionally
- at 922 Marisa Ln and 1323 Amethyst St
- when I am at peace with myself

ⓒ

ⓓ

home

Notes:
I love my "homes".
I know I'm blessed.

FOR OFFICIAL USE ONLY

I don't think my idea of "home" is the same as many people's. Because I don't own a home and I'm recently out of college, I've moved a lot in the past few years. Instead of concentrating on a physical place, I broadened the idea of "home" to include the many things shown here. Also, the masking tape and funky tags add a fun touch to the page to keep it from being too serious or traditional.

Jessica Fulkerson

Alison

Jessie

Michelle

Sarah

Linda

CONTRIB-UTORS

Alison Flynn lives in France but loves to go home to the States for iced tea and Goldfish crackers. She started scrapbooking about four years ago. She's been doing the Dares since the very first one because they make her look at things from an angle she would never have come up with on her own.

Jessica Fulkerson started scrapping over three years ago in college and is now documenting her life since graduation, out in "the real world." Jessica was attracted to the Dares for their edginess, which isn't commonplace in the scrapbooking world. She loved that they encourage what she always believed in doing—scrapping without rules. Her passion is documenting stories. She enjoys the artistic, creative side of scrapping, but in the end she hopes each of her pages has a true core to it. She finds inspiration in her everyday from graffiti on L.A. streets to a lyric from her favorite punk rock band.

Sarah Bowen has been scrapping since 2003, but scrapping her own style since 2005. She loves the unexpected—the little surprises are what make life memorable. Her favorite subjects to scrap are places and things that hold true and strong memories. People are sometimes secondary in her pages, a little unorthodox, but that's how she likes it.

Sarah started doing the Dares in 2006 as a weekly jumpstart for her creativity. Each topic and viewpoint is so genuine and inspiring. The Dares help her dig deep and really create pages that are truly meaningful and heartfelt.

Michelle Guray resides in Corona, California, and has been married to her best friend, Allan, for ten years. She's a stay-at-home mom to two children, Aidan (6) and Mia (1), who are her favorite subjects. She began scrapbooking after the birth of her son and enjoys this hobby not only as a way to capture memories but also as a creative outlet. The Dares offer

a wealth of inspiration and participating in the challenges has given her the extra push to create more meaningful layouts. In her spare time, Michelle loves reading magazines, shopping at Target and going to the movies.

Linda Buranasakorn lives in southern California with her awesome family. She loves to scrap because it's fun and creative. She loves to laugh and is a fan of sarcasm and chicken salad sandwiches. Linda started scrapbooking in 2003, and while it was fun, she wasn't a fan of "the rules." You know the ones. She discovered the Dares, and dug their creativity, their challenges, their inspiration. Some of her favorites aspects of scrapping include the friends she's made and the stretching of her imagination. Linda is a fan of little bits. Bits + Memories + Paper + Photos = Visual Log of Her Life.

Jamaica

Jamie

Laura

Erica

Anja

Jill

Jamaica Edgell lives on the central coast of California with her longtime boyfriend and kitty. She wears flip-flops all year long and spends her days as a designer, making things pretty for work. Paper-obsessed, Jamaica hoards office supplies, letter-pressed greeting cards and anything flocked. She daydreams about crafting and schemes of new ways to convert her friends to scrapbooking. She loves doing the Dares because they're quirky and thoughtful and fun...and because they make scrapbooking cool.

Erica Hernandez lives a quiet life with her husband and two young sons. She has been scrapbooking for almost five years and is most grateful for all the friendships she's developed as a result.

Jamie Bagley lives in Colorado and loves the crazy weather, although she lives for the summer when she can ride her scooter around town. Scrapping is her "Zen" activity where she can zone out and go to town. Jamie loves ranch dressing, her niece, and polka dots to distraction. She loves the Dares so much for opening her eyes and forcing her to think a little more. Thanks to the Dares, Jamie has scrapped about things she never would've thought of, and she's so pleased to see those pages in her albums. Jamie hopes to continue to feel inspired by everything around her and have the most fun doing it!

Anja Wade lives in Warren, Maryland, and has been scrapbooking for seven years. She has a background in chemistry and teaches at the high school and college level. She loves the creative outlet provided by scrapbooking—it gives her the chance to use her artistic side and helps her feel balanced. When she's not scrapbooking, she enjoys cooking, reading, running, going to the gym, and spending time with family and friends.

Laura Kurz lives in Baltimore with her husband Ken and their golden retriever, Charmer. She works in the public relations field and enjoys spending summer weekends at the beach with friends and family. Laura has been scrapbooking in some form from an early age, starting with cutting up her extra family photos in kindergarten, graduating to making photo collages for college, and then discovering scrapbooking in its current form in 2004.

Jill Hornby is a 24-year-old wife and mom. She started scrapbooking after her daughter Lia was born in 2005. Jill strives to create scrapbook pages that have a real story behind them and that capture the beauty and happiness in everyday life. The Dares are awesome because they give Jill a jumping-off point for her pages, and they inspire her to scrapbook about more than just the developmental milestones of her one-year-old.

SUPPLIES

Page 10: Positive Self Talk

In With The Good — Genevieve Simmonds
Supplies: Cardstock; acrylic paint; letter stickers (EK Success); rub-on accents (7gypsies, My Mind's Eye); rub-on letters (Autumn Leaves); sticker accents (7gypsies)

Restroom Confessional — Jessica Fulkerson
Supplies: Cardstock; patterned paper (KI Memories); chipboard letters (Heidi Swapp); tags (Making Memories); rub-on accent (7gypsies); Triumph Tippa font (Dafont)

Be Proud — Kristina Contes
Supplies: Kraft cardstock; patterned vellum, rub-on letters (Hambly); acrylic paint; ledger paper (Making Memories); epoxy sticker (EK Success); drywall tape (Home Depot); stamp (Stampers Anonymous); solvent ink; Verdana font (Microsoft)

Repeat (As Needed) — Nisa Fiin
Supplies: Cardstock; patterned paper (My Mind's Eye); rub-on accents (Hambly); dye ink; acrylic paint; paper punches (Marvy); eyelets, label maker; staples

Page 12: Safe Place

Pinch Me — Genevieve Simmonds
Supplies: Cardstock; patterned paper (7gypsies, American Crafts); rub-on letters (Autumn Leaves, BasicGrey); photo corner (Heidi Swapp); pen

Rule #1 — Kristina Contes
Supplies: Patterned paper (7gypsies, Chatterbox, Making Memories, Wooster and Prince); cork paper (Karen Foster); decorative tape (7gypsies); rub-on letters (Autumn Leaves); rub-on accents (Hambly); stamps (7gypsies, Purple Onion); solvent ink; embossing powder; pen

My Strength — Meghan Heath Dymock
Supplies: Cardstock; chipboard letters and star (Heidi Swapp); rub-on accents (Autumn Leaves, Heidi Swapp, KI Memories); foil wings (PaperArtsy); stickers (Making Memories); stamps (Ma Vinci); quote tag (My Mind's Eye); solvent ink; rhinestones, transparency (unknown)

Get Away — Nisa Fiin
Supplies: Patterned paper (7gypsies, BasicGrey, KI Memories, Making Memories); rub-on accents (Hambly); stamps (Technique Tuesday); dye ink; brads, concho (Making Memories, Scrapworks); pen; staples

Page 14: Obsessed

Currently Cranberry — Nisa Fiin
Supplies: Patterned paper (KI Memories); stamps (Purple Onion); solvent ink; digital brush (Designer Digitals); pen

Fresh Clean Rubber — Genevieve Simmonds
Supplies: Cardstock; stamps (Lazar); letter stickers (Chatterbox); sticker accents (7gypsies)

Real World — Jamie Bagley
Supplies: Patterned paper (Chatterbox, SEI); letter stickers (Doodlebug); acrylic paint; decorative tape (7gypsies); stars (Sandylion); rub-on accent (KI Memories); tag (unknown); masking tape; pen

City Dates — Kristina Contes
Supplies: Cardstock; patterned paper (Karen Foster); map (MTA); corrugated cardboard; stamps (7gypsies, FontWerks, Hampton Art); corner rounder; solvent ink

Pge 16: Favorites

Lia's Favorite Things — Jill Hornby
Supplies: Cardstock; patterned paper (American Crafts, Crate Paper, Scenic Route); acrylic paint; stamps (EK Success, FontWerks); dye ink; fabric (unknown); staples; thread; HammerKeys font (Internet download)

Favorites — Meghan Heath Dymock
Supplies: Patterned paper (Rusty Pickle); letter stickers (Autumn Leaves); rub-on accents (Autumn Leaves, Heidi Swapp, My Mind's Eye); rhinestones (My Mind's Eye); pen

C — Kristina Contes
Supplies: Cardboard; patterned paper (7gypsies, Chatterbox); patterned transparencies (Hambly); envelopes (Waste Not); chipboard letters (Fancy Pants, Heidi Swapp); index cards, sticker accents (7gypsies); labels (Paper Source); charm (Artgirlz); ribbon (Chatterbox, M&J); stamps (FontWerks, Hampton Art, Purple Onion); book rings; pen

Indirectly Inherited — Nisa Fiin
Supplies: Patterned paper (BasicGrey, My Mind's Eye, KI Memories, Mustard Moon); rub-on letters (Hambly); ribbon (May Arts); chipboard (Heidi Swapp); dye ink; decorative punches (EK Success); pen; Century Gothic font (Microsoft)

Page 18: Bling

K — Kristina Contes
Supplies: Cardstock; chipboard letter, rhinestone (Heidi Swapp); letter stamps (FontWerks, PSX); stamping ink; crystals (Swarovski); rub-on accents (Hambly); ribbons (M&J); pen

The Story — Laura Kurz
Supplies: Patterned paper (Autumn Leaves, Chatterbox); stamp (FontWerks); rub-on letters (Making Memories); rhinestones (Heidi Swapp)

Cute Hair — Genevieve Simmonds
Supplies: Patterned paper (7gypsies); letter stickers (Autumn Leaves, Chatterbox); glitter glue (Ranger); rhinestones (unknown); acrylic paint; pen

Truth — Meghan Heath Dymock
Supplies: Cardstock; chipboard letters, decorative tape, rhinestones, sticker accents (Heidi Swapp); stamp (River City Rubber Works); flower (Prima); rub-on accents (7gypsies, Autumn Leaves); sticker accent (EK Success); photo corner; pen

Page 20: Where I Grew Up

Transatlantic — Alison Flynn
Supplies: Cardstock; patterned paper (7gypsies, Autumn Leaves); brads, rub-on letters (American Crafts); ribbon (American Crafts, Jo-Ann, Strano); stamp (Close to My Heart); tag (7gypsies); corner rounder; stamping ink; pen; Diesel font (Misprinted Type)

Another Time, Another Place — Anja Wade
Supplies: Cardstock; acrylic paint; patterned paper (Anna Griffin); number stickers (American Crafts); floss; buttons, flowers, folder tab, leaves, sequins (unknown)

My City — Genevieve Simmonds
Supplies: Cardstock; patterned paper (unknown); watermark ink; gesso; rub-on and sticker accents (7gypsies); pen

120 — Laura Kurz
Supplies: Patterned paper (7gypsies, American Crafts, Sassafras Lass); chipboard letter (BasicGrey); stamps (FontWerks); number rub-ons (American Crafts); brads (Around the Block); Times New Roman font (Microsoft)

In These Woods — Nisa Fiin
Supplies: Cardstock; patterned paper (PaperGami); patterned overlay (My Mind's Eye); stamps (Federal Stamp and Seal, Purple Onion); ribbon (May Arts); grape vine; tag; wire; staples; pen

Dysfunctional Love — Kristina Contes
Supplies: Cardstock; patterned paper (Scrapworks); transparency (Hambly); chipboard letters (Heidi Swapp); rub-on letters (Autumn Leaves, Heidi Swapp, Making Memories); acrylic paint; sticker accent (7gypsies); pen

Page 24: Accomplishments

Our Baby — Kristina Contes
Supplies: Cardstock; patterned paper (Scenic Route); rub-on letters (Autumn Leaves); sticker accents (Chatterbox); frame (Li'l Davis); dye ink; brads (Bazzill); pen

Looks Like We Made It — Linda Buranasakorn
Supplies: Patterned paper (Li'l Davis); letter stamps (Autumn Leaves); rub-on letters (American Crafts); rub-on accents (BasicGrey, Chatterbox); ribbon (BasicGrey); heart accent (Heidi Swapp); stamping ink; sticker accents (Creative Imaginations); stamp (Stampin' Up); pen

We're Just Getting Started —
Meghan Heath Dymock
Supplies: Cardstock; stamps (Ma Vinci's, Purple Onion); sticker accents (7gypsies, American Crafts, K&Co.); star accent (Heidi Swapp); pen

Boot Camp Kav — Nisa Fiin
Supplies: Cardstock; patterned paper (KI Memories); metal letter (American Crafts); ribbon (Chatterbox); acrylic paint; dye ink; corner punch; cardboard; wire; staples

Page 28: Hard

I'm Still Sad — Genevieve Simmonds
Supplies: Cardstock; patterned paper (K&Co.); word stickers (Magnetic Poetry); mesh (Magic Mesh); journaling sticker (Heidi Swapp); stamps (7gypsies, FontWerks); staples; pen

Just Chill — Kristina Contes
Supplies: Patterned paper (7gypsies, Hambly, Making Memories, Paper Presentation); letter stamps (PSX); word stamp (FontWerks); stamping ink; letter stickers (Scrapworks); pen

I Need This — Nisa Fiin
Supplies: Patterned paper (Autumn Leaves, BasicGrey, KI Memories, Sandylion); rub-on and sticker accents (7gypsies); stamps (Li'l Davis, Making Memories); acrylic paint; dye ink; tag, ticket stub (unknown); pen

Open Your Eyes — Meghan Heath Dymock
Supplies: Cardstock; patterned paper (7gypsies); letter stickers (Heidi Swapp); sticker accents (Wal-Mart); rub-on accents (7gypsies, Making Memories); stamp (FontWerks); stamping ink; ribbon (unknown); pen

Page 30: Guilty Pleasures

So In Love — Kristina Contes
Supplies: Cardboard (Ink Pad); patterned paper (Kate's Paperie); stamps (FontWerks); embossing powder (Ranger); rub-on accents (7gypsies); label (Paper Source); beads, wire thread (unknown); pencil

Yum — Genevieve Simmonds
Supplies: Patterned paper (American Crafts, Autumn Leaves); chipboard letters (Heidi Swapp); stamps (FontWerks); pigment ink; acrylic paint; pen

Not Too Guilty Pleasure —
Meghan Heath Dymock
Supplies: Patterned paper, rub-on accents, transparency frame (My Mind's Eye); letter stickers (KI Memories, SEI); rhinestones (Junkitz); sticker accents (Autumn Leaves)

So Obsessed — Jamie Bagley
Supplies: Patterned paper (KI Memories); ledger paper (Making Memories); rub-on letters (EK Success); rub-on accents (BasicGrey, EK Success); stamps (Autumn Leaves, Heidi Swapp); stamping ink; label, star stickers (3M); rickrack (Doodlebug); pen

Page 32: Fear

Relinquishing Control — Genevieve Simmonds
Supplies: Patterned paper (7gypsies); rub-on letters (Autumn Leaves, Chatterbox, Dollar Store); sticker accent (Heidi Grace); stamps (Lazar); dye ink; pen

This is Fact Not Fiction —
Meghan Heath Dymock
Supplies: Cardstock; acrylic paint; decorative tape (Heidi Swapp); pins (Heidi Grace); pen; lyrics (Death Cab for Cutie)

Pros/Cons — Kristina Contes
Supplies: Envelopes (Waste Not); letter stickers (Making Memories); sticker accents (7gypsies); stamps (Catslife Press, Purple Onion); embossing powder; pen

Fears — Michelle Guray
Supplies: Cardstock; patterned paper (My Mind's Eye); chipboard letters (Heidi Swapp); rub-on accents (American Crafts); digital lace brush, photo edge brush (Two Peas in a Bucket)

As Good A Mother — Sarah Bowen
Supplies: Cardstock; patterned paper (Ali Edwards, BasicGrey, Creative Imaginations, KI Memories, Mustard Moon); gesso; tab (7gypsies); letter stickers (American Crafts); diamond glaze; pen

Don't Want This Story to End — Nisa Fiin
Supplies: Patterned paper (7gypsies); letter stickers (Headline Sign); stamp (FontWerks); dye ink; ribbon (American Crafts, May Arts); notebook paper; heart accent (Heidi Swapp); staples; pen

Page 36: Fights

Still Fighting It — Nisa Fiin
Supplies: Patterned paper (7gypsies, My Mind's Eye); transparency frame (My Mind's Eye); ribbon (May Arts); sticker accents (7gypsies); stamps (Purple Onion); dye ink; acrylic paint; postcard (unknown); staples; pen

I Fight With Best Friends —
Meghan Heath Dymock
Supplies: Cardstock; acrylic paint; felt flower, foil stickers (unknown); pen

Scared — Kristina Contes
Supplies: Cardstock; patterned paper (Paper Source); letter stickers (Making Memories, Paper Source); ribbon (M&J); rub-on accents (BasicGrey); corner rounder; staples

It's Called Parenting — Genevieve Simmonds
Supplies: Patterned paper, embroidered appliqué (Autumn Leaves); stamps (7gypsies, FontWerks); pigment ink; felt; staples; pen

Page 38: Regrets

Too Few Photos of You — Nisa Fiin
Supplies: Cardstock; patterned paper (7gypsies, Hambly, KI Memories, My Mind's Eye); ribbon (American Crafts); rub-on accents (My Mind's Eye); corner punch; notebook paper; map (unknown); pen

I Wish For More — Genevieve Simmonds
Supplies: Patterned paper (Lazar); fabric (Amy Butler); buttons (Autumn Leaves); letter stickers (Making Memories); stamps (Purple Onion); thread; vinyl pocket (unknown); dye ink; pen

All My Regrets are Subjective —
Meghan Heath Dymock
Supplies: Cardstock; rub-on letters and accents (Autumn Leaves); sticker accents (EK Success); pen

Art School Drop Out — Kristina Contes
Supplies: Corrugated cardboard (Paper Company); patterned paper (Chatterbox, Scrapworks); letter stickers (Avery, KI Memories); ribbon (Scrapworks); rub-on accent (Hambly); beads (unknown); photo corners (Canson); Kingthings Trypwriter font (Internet download)

Page 40: Make a Mess

Photos Reborn — Nisa Fiin
Supplies: Cardstock; patterned paper (Cavallini); ribbon (May Arts); sticker accents (7gypsies, Paper Source); dye ink; digital brush (Rhonna Designs); acrylic paint; staples; text book pages; pen; Book Antigua font (Microsoft); Witchcraft font (Internet download)

Almost Too Much — Jill Hornby
Supplies: Cardstock; acrylic paints; rub-on accents (KI Memories); fabric (unknown); staples; thread; pen

Personal Expression — Kristina Contes
Supplies: Cardstock; acrylic paint; patterned paper (7gypsies, dictionary clippings, Roger la Borde); chipboard letters (BasicGrey); letter stickers (Making Memories); crystals (Swarovski); ribbon (M&J); stamps (7gypsies, FontWerks); pen

Burn This City — Jessica Fulkerson
Supplies: Cardstock; cardboard; acrylic paint; tags (Making Memories); sticker accents (7gypsies); Broken Wing font (Internet download)

Page 44: Imperfect Photo

Perpetual Motion — Anja Wade
Supplies: Cardstock; patterned paper (BasicGrey); rub-on letters (American Crafts, Scrapworks); corner rounder; floss; pen

Joycam — Genevieve Simmonds
Supplies: Patterned paper (KI Memories); letter stamps (FontWerks); accent stamps (Autumn Leaves); staples; dimensional foam; pen

A Blur — Jamaica Edgell
Supplies: Patterned paper (7gypsies, Paper Source); ribbons (Lina G'); staples; Angelina font (Internet download)

Our Little Lady — Kristina Contes
Supplies: Cardstock; patterned paper (Roger La Borde); rub-on letters (Hambly); rub-on accents (My Mind's Eye); ribbon (May Arts); bookplate (Making Memories); brads

Privacy — Meghan Heath Dymock
Supplies: Cardstock; patterned paper (7gypsies, Making Memories); photo corners, rhinestones (Heidi Swapp); acrylic heart (Heidi Grace); envelope (Li'l Davis); stamps (Purple Onion); tag (Autumn Leaves); acrylic paint; transparent tag (Creative Imaginations); sticker accents (7gypsies); pen

Click — Nisa Fiin
Supplies: Patterned paper (7gypsies, Making Memories, My Mind's Eye, SEI); chipboard letters (Scenic Route); sticker accents (7gypsies); stamps (Purple Onion); dye ink; circle punch; pen

Beautiful Wedding, Bad Photographer — Laura Kurz
Supplies: Cardstock; rub-on letters (American Crafts); patterned transparency (My Mind's Eye); rub-on accent (BasicGrey); staples; Century Gothic font (Microsoft)

Page 48: Distress

Sandbox Garden — Nisa Fiin
Supplies: Patterned paper (Rusty Pickle); digital brushes (Design Fruit); rub-on accents (My Mind's Eye); dye ink; ledger paper; pen; Rough Draft font (Internet download)

A Few Things — Jamie Bagley
Supplies: Patterned paper (Déjà Views); survey (magazine advertisement); masking tape; clear frame (Making Memories); star stickers (3M); word quotes (unknown); stamping ink; pen

Urban Grunge — Sarah Bowen
Supplies: Cardstock; patterned paper (BasicGrey, Chatterbox, KI Memories, Mustard Moon); scotch tape; rub-on accents (BasicGrey); date stamp (Wal-Mart); key (unknown); chalk; letter stickers (American Crafts, Making Memories); acrylic paint; gesso; walnut ink; thread; pen

My Best — Kristina Contes
Supplies: Cardstock; cardboard; stamps (Lazar, Rubber Baby); embossing powder (Ranger); letter stickers (Heidi Swapp); corner rounder; staples; Verdana font (Microsoft)

Page 50: The Worst Thing

In My Head — Nisa Fiin
Supplies: Patterned paper (7gypsies, Autumn Leaves); number stickers (Headline Sign); rub-on accent (Letraset); pen

I Couldn't Save You — Meghan Heath Dymock
Photo by: Tyson Dymock
Supplies: Cardstock; rhinestones (Heidi Swapp); rub-on accent (Autumn Leaves); letter stickers (Making Memories); pen

The Ice Queen — Jamaica Edgell
Supplies: Textured paper (Gmund Valentinoise); sequins; Mom's Typewriter font (Internet download)

Me — Kristina Contes
Supplies: Patterned paper (7gypsies); cardboard; letter stickers (Making Memories); photo corners; pen

Page 52: Pissed Off

Grr... — Kristina Contes
Supplies: Cardstock; cardboard; rub-on letters (American Crafts, Hambly); sticker accents (7gypsies, K&Co.); decorative tape (Heidi Swapp); stamp (Purple Onion); solvent ink; brads; ribbon (M&J); subway map; dictionary clippings

Liar, Liar — Jessica Fulkerson
Supplies: Patterned paper (KI Memories); transparent letters (Heidi Swapp); sticker accents (7gypsies); tags (Making Memories); chipboard accent (Deluxe Designs); decorative tape (Chatterbox); brad; pen; Broken Wing font (Internet download)

She Gets Bent — Genevieve Simmonds
Supplies: Patterned paper (Making Memories, Polar Bear Press); stamp (FontWerks); gesso; watermark ink; masking tape; pen; Letter Gothic Standard font (Internet download)

Pissed Off Finds Me — Meghan Heath Dymock
Supplies: Cardstock; patterned paper (Autumn Leaves); wax; gold foil stickers (unknown); sticker accent (EK Success); walnut ink; lined paper

Page 54: Mortified

Until Then — Genevieve Simmonds
Supplies: Patterned paper (SEI); decorative tape, journaling accents (Heidi Swapp); acrylic stickers (Colorbök); brads; pen

Little Things — Jamie Bagley
Supplies: Patterned paper (SEI); acrylic paint; flower and letter masks (Heidi Swapp); pen

Hey Dork — Kristina Contes
Supplies: Cardstock; patterned paper (Chatterbox, KI Memories); stamps (FontWerks, Technique Tuesday); rub-on accents (American Crafts, BasicGrey); ribbon (M&J); transparency; staples; Times New Roman font (Microsoft)

Ben @ 10 — Nisa Fiin
Supplies: Patterned paper (7gypsies, Anna Griffin, Chatterbox, My Mind's Eye); decorative tape (Heidi Swapp); stamps (Purple Onion); dye ink; brad, photo turn (7gypsies); Scrabble tile (Hasbro); pen

Page 58: Permission Slip

Ready to Fly — Michelle Guray
Supplies: Cardstock; watercolor paper (Strathmore); letter stickers (American Crafts, EK Success, K&Co.); acrylic paint; wing accent (Scrapartist); paper flowers (Doodlebug); pen

Attn: Haters — Kristina Contes
Supplies: Cardstock; patterned paper (7gypsies, Making Memories, Paper Presentation, Paper Source, Scenic Route); tab (SEI); ribbon (May Arts); crystals (Swarovski); stamps (FontWerks, Stampers Anonymous); pigment and solvent ink; staples; pen

Mess/Break — Genevieve Simmonds
Supplies: Cardstock; acrylic paints; watermark ink; staples; pen

Stop Worrying — Nisa Fiin
Supplies: Patterned paper (My Mind's Eye, Scenic Route); letter stickers (Headline Sign); rub-on accents (Chatterbox); stamps (FontWerks); dye ink; adhesive foam; sandpaper; pen

Stay Real — Meghan Heath Dymock
Supplies: Cardstock; decorative tape (7gypsies); patterned transparency (Hambly); letter stickers (Heidi Swapp); wing accents (PaperArtsy); rhinestones; sticker accent (Making Memories); flower, monogram letter (unknown); pen

Permission to be Human — Sarah Bowen
Supplies: Watercolor paper; watercolor paint; pen

Page 62: Shoes

New Shoes — Nisa Fiin
Supplies: Patterned paper (Daisy D's, K&Co., Karen Foster, My Mind's Eye); letter stickers (Headline Sign); sticker accents (7gypsies); dye ink; ledger paper; pen

My Favorite Shoes — Sarah Bowen
Supplies: Patterned paper, ribbon, rub-on accents (BasicGrey); transparency; acrylic paint; gesso; staples; masking tape; letter punches (Making Memories); star accents (Heidi Swapp); gaffer tape (7gypsies); walnut ink; acrylic letter (unknown); pen; 1942 Report, California, Porcelain fonts (Internet download); Century Gothic font (Microsoft)

ADD Kickin' in Hardcore — Kristina Contes
Supplies: Patterned paper (FontWerks, SEI); patterned transparency (Hambly); letter stickers (Heidi Swapp, Making Memories); letter stamps (FontWerks, PSX); pigment and solvent ink; ribbon (M&J); notebook paper; pen

Fantasy vs. Reality — Genevieve Simmonds
Supplies: Cardstock; patterned paper (Lazar); sticker accents (Provo Craft); pen; AL Fantasy, Another Typewriter fonts (Internet download)

Page 64: Little Me

Sometimes I Wish I Was Six — Nisa Fiin
Supplies: Patterned paper (7gypsies, Autumn Leaves, My Mind's Eye); circle accent, plastic letters (Heidi Swapp); sticker accents (7gypsies, Paper Source); dye ink; wing accents (PaperArtsy); pen

Peter Rabbit is Still Alive — Genevieve Simmonds
Supplies: Patterned paper, rub-on accents (My Mind's Eye); rub-on letters (Making Memories); stamps (7gypsies); corner rounder

Joshie & Jaime — Jamaica Edgell
Supplies: Cardstock; transparency; index tab (Avery); ribbon (Lina G'); staples; pen

Friends Forever — Meghan Heath Dymock
Supplies: Patterned paper (A2Z); sticker accents (7gypsies, K&Co., Making Memories); decorative tape, transparent frame (Heidi Swapp); rub-on accents (Autumn Leaves, Heidi Swapp); acrylic paint; stamps (Purple Onion); stamping ink; pen

My Golden Girl — Laura Kurz
Supplies: Cardstock; acrylic paint; letter stickers (Making Memories); rub-on accent (BasicGrey); Times New Roman font (Microsoft)

Do Not — Kristina Contes
Supplies: Cardstock; patterned paper (Kate's Paperie); patterned transparency (Hambly); ribbon, rickrack (M&J); letter stickers (Heidi Swapp); sticker and rub-on accents (7gypsies); stamp (Purple Onion); sandpaper; Times New Roman font (Microsoft)

Little Girl — Anja Wade
Supplies: Kraft cardstock; cardstock; letter stickers (Heidi Swapp); label (C-Line); floss; felt accent (Making Memories); sticker accent (EK Success); digital brush (Design Fruit); corner rounder; pen

Page 68: One Sentence

I Still Don't Know — Alison Flynn
Supplies: Cardstock; letter stickers (Making Memories); labels (7gypsies, Li'l Davis); stamps (Hero Arts, Leave Memories); stamping ink; masking tape; rubber bands; staples; acrylic paint; mesh (Magic Mesh); pencil; pen

I Am Spent — Genevieve Simmonds
Supplies: Patterned paper (Heidi Grace); letter stamps (Li'l Davis); accent stamps (Purple Onion); pigment ink; acrylic paint; twill (Autumn Leaves); pen

Confuse Them — Kristina Contes
Supplies: Cardstock; patterned paper (Making Memories, SEI); rub-on letters (Autumn Leaves, My Mind's Eye); letter stickers (Heidi Swapp, Making Memories); sticker accent (7gypsies); stamps (FontWerks); stamping ink; corner rounder; pen

One of Us — Nisa Fiin
Supplies: Cardstock; patterned paper (BasicGrey, Fancy Pants); chipboard letters, rub-on accents (Chatterbox); ribbon (May Arts); stamps (Autumn Leaves, Purple Onion); solvent ink; pen

Page 70: Swap

The Jack — Genevieve Simmonds
Supplies: Patterned paper (Making Memories); letter stickers (Me & My Big Ideas); sticker accents (Artchix, Heidi Swapp); stamp (Purple Onion); pen

5 Times — Kristina Contes
Supplies: Cardstock; patterned paper (7gypsies, Ali Edwards, Kate's Paperie); chipboard letters, letter stickers (Heidi Swapp); stamps (7gypsies, FontWerks); rub-on accents (7gypsies, My Mind's Eye); solvent ink; ribbon (May Arts); crystals (Swarovski); measuring tape; Times New Roman font (Microsoft)

Two Nuks — Nisa Fiin
Supplies: Cardstock; patterned paper (7gypsies, Chatterbox, Hambly, My Mind's Eye); decorative tape (7gypsies); stamps (Autumn Leaves); solvent ink; ticket stubs (unknown); digital brush (Lazar); pen

Gracie — Meghan Heath Dymock
Supplies: Cardstock; acrylic paint; chipboard letters, rhinestones (Heidi Swapp); label, star accent (Li'l Davis); letter stickers (Autumn Leaves, Making Memories); photo corners

Page 72: Date

She Traveled to Italy —
Meghan Heath Dymock
Supplies: Patterned paper (Rusty Pickle); letter stickers (Making Memories); photo corners, plastic letters, rhinestones (Heidi Swapp); stamp (English Stamp Co.); acrylic paint; sticker accents (K&Co.); pen

Thanksgiving 2000 — Jamaica Edgell
Supplies: Patterned paper (Kate's Paperie); patterned transparency (Hambly); rub-on letters (Heidi Swapp); ribbons (Lina G'); staples; pen

Road Trip To Me — Nisa Fiin
Supplies: Cardstock; patterned paper (My Mind's Eye); ribbon (May Arts); rub-on accents (Chatterbox); stickers accents (7gypsies, Chatterbox); stamps (Purple Onion); dye ink; map; mesh; staples; pen

08.26.2006 — Genevieve Simmonds
Supplies: Cardstock; rub-on accents (7gypsies, BasicGrey); lace; dye ink; Letter Gothic Standard font (Internet download)

Page 74: Ribbon

Chloe Rose — Kristina Contes
Supplies: Cardstock; patterned transparency (Hambly); chipboard letters (Heidi Swapp); ribbons (Chatterbox, Doodlebug, M&J, May Arts, Scrapworks); sticker accents (EK Success); crystals (Swarovski)

Husband & Wife — Jamaica Edgell
Supplies: Cardstock; ribbon (Lina G', Ribbon Jar); rub-on words (Déjà Views)

ABCs — Genevieve Simmonds
Supplies: Cardstock; patterned paper, twill (Autumn Leaves); Tia Doodle Birdies, Viva, Vivaldi fonts (Internet download)

Luckiest — Nisa Fiin
Supplies: Cardstock; patterned paper (Creative Imaginations); ribbon (American Crafts, Chatterbox, May Arts, Strano); sticker accents (Cavallini); dog accent (Memories in the Making); staples; pen

Page 78: Seven Random Facts

M&T Style — Meghan Heath Dymock
Photo by: Nisa Fiin
Supplies: Patterned paper (Making Memories); letter stamps (FontWerks); rhinestones, rub-on accents, star accents (Heidi Swapp); number accents (7gypsies); stamps (Purple Onion); pen

This One Moment — Alison Flynn
Supplies: Digital patterned paper (Two Peas); digital brushes (Adobe Photoshop, Design Fruit, Erica Hernandez); digital elements (Adobe); ISketchy Times, JP Hand, Misproject fonts (Internet download)

This Boy — Nisa Fiin
Supplies: Patterned paper (Adornit); ribbon (May Arts); sticker accents (7gypsies); stamps (Purple Onion); dye ink; notch tool; digital brush (Lazar); Scrabble tile (Hasbro); staples; Century Gothic font (Microsoft)

All Random — Genevieve Simmonds
Supplies: Patterned paper (BasicGrey); letter stickers (Making Memories); journaling accents (Heidi Swapp); rub-on accents (7gypsies); sticker accents (Die Cuts With A View); pen; AL Typewriter font (Internet download)

7 Random Facts — Kristina Contes
Supplies: Patterned transparency (Hambly); envelope (Knock Knock); chipboard letters (Heidi Swapp); number stickers (Heidi Swapp, Making Memories); stamp (Purple Onion); ribbon (M&J); solvent ink; brad; crystals (Swarovski); staples; pen

7 — Michelle Guray
Supplies: Patterned paper and transparency (Hambly); rub-on accent (Heidi Swapp); labels (Li'l Davis); decorative tape (7gypsies); date stamp (unknown); staples

7 Random Facts — Jill Hornby
Supplies: Cardstock; acrylic paint; floss; pen

Page 82: Found Object

Make Sure It's Fun To Watch — Jamie Bagley
Supplies: Patterned paper (SEI); bird accent, word bubble (Bam Pop); rub-on accents (7gypsies, BasicGrey, Doodlebug); arrow and title (found in magazine); solvent ink; pen

Life in a Nutshell — Nisa Fiin
Supplies: Kraft cardstock; stamps (FontWerks); solvent ink; staples; die-cut wallet sheet; pen

Remember That Day? — Genevieve Simmonds
Supplies: Cardstock; letter and accent stamps (FontWerks); word stickers (EK Success); sticker border (KI Memories)

Las Vegas Elevator — Meghan Heath Dymock
Supplies: Chipboard; word plaque (unknown); rhinestones (Heidi Swapp); dye ink; twine; pen

Moments — Kristina Contes
Supplies: Clay pot (Williams-Sonoma); corrugated cardboard; patterned paper (7gypsies, BasicGrey, Hambly, Karen Foster, Making Memories, Paper Source, Roger la Borde, SEI); stamp accents (FontWerks, Purple Onion); sticker accents (7gypsies, Doodlebug, EK Success, Heidi Swapp); rub-on accents (BasicGrey, Hambly); ribbon (American Crafts, M&J, May Arts, Michaels, Scrapworks); rhinestones; pen

Page 84: Fierce

Fierce — Nisa Fiin
Supplies: Cardstock; patterned paper (American Crafts, Design Originals, Making Memories); ribbon (May Arts); stamp and sticker accents (7gypsies); dye ink; acrylic paint; chipboard letter (Heidi Swapp); brads; pen

Oh, and P.S. — Genevieve Simmonds
Supplies: Cardstock; fabric (unknown); thread; corner rounder; pen; Prestige Elise Standard, Uncle Typewriter fonts (Internet download)

NYC — Kristina Contes
Supplies: Corrugated cardboard; subway map; dictionary clippings; magazine clippings; letter stickers (Heidi Swapp); rub-on accents (Hambly)

Scream — Meghan Heath Dymock
Supplies: Cardstock; rub-on letters (Making Memories); stamps (Purple Onion); chipboard letter, clock accent (Heidi Swapp); gold accents (PaperArtsy); red metal accents, rub-on accents (7gypsies); sticker accents (Making Memories); rhinestone

Page 86: Things I Do

10:30 Sushi — Genevieve Simmonds
Supplies: Cardstock; patterned paper (Anna Griffin); letter stickers (Heidi Grace, Making Memories); letter stamps (EK Success); word stickers (7gypsies); stamp (FontWerks); business card; chopstick wrapper; staples

Things I Do No. 9 — Kristina Contes
Supplies: Cardstock; patterned paper (SEI); rub-on letters (American Crafts); rub-on accents (BasicGrey, Hambly); letter stickers (Making Memories); decorative tape (Heidi Swapp); dye ink; pen; CD cover (Beastie Boys)

Things I Do... — Nisa Fiin
Supplies: Patterned paper (7gypsies, Around the Block, Autumn Leaves, Mustard Moon); rub-on accents (K&Co.); decorative tape (7gypsies); photo corner (Chatterbox); stamps (Purple Onion); solvent ink; digital brush (Lazar); pen

Things You Do — Jill Hornby
Supplies: Cardstock; patterned paper (Cactus Pink, Old Navy, SEI); letter stickers (KI Memories); arrow (Old Navy); journaling accent (Heidi Swapp); fabric, lace, star accent (unknown); ribbon (Jo-Ann's); staples; thread

Page 88: Note

Husbands & Children & Swing Sets — Nisa Fiin
Supplies: Patterned paper (Anna Griffin, Chatterbox); ribbon (May Arts); rub-on accent (7gypsies); adhesive foam; stamps (Purple Onion); dye ink; photo corner (Scrapworks); notebook paper; staples; pen; Stylus font (Internet download)

Love Letter — Linda Buranasakorn
Supplies: Cardstock; patterned paper (Doodlebug); letter stickers (American Crafts); letter stamps (Stampin' Up); stamping ink; heart sticker (unknown); staples; typewriter

Love Notes From My J — Kristina Contes
Supplies: Folder (Globe-Weis); letter stickers (EK Success, Heidi Swapp); rub-on letters (American Crafts); rub-on definitions (7gypsies); dye ink; photo corners (Canson)

Year Four — Meghan Heath Dymock
Supplies: Cardstock; patterned paper (7gypsies); letter stickers, photo corners (Heidi Swapp); patterned transparency (Hambly); decorative tape (7gypsies); velvet magnet (EK Success); metal accent (unknown); flower (Junkitz); paint, sticker accents (Making Memories)

Vegas Baby, Vegas — Genevieve Simmonds
Supplies: Patterned paper (7gypsies, BasicGrey); letter stamps (Purple Onion); pigment ink; letter stickers (EK Success); lace (unknown); staples; hotel note paper; pen

Thundercats — Anja Wade
Supplies: Patterned paper (KI Memories); letter stamps (unknown); dye ink; label (C-Line); tab (7gypsies); floss; pipe cleaner; staples

Page 92: Uniform

Everyday Hoodies — Nisa Fiin
Supplies: Patterned paper (Hambly); chipboard letters (Heidi Swapp); ribbon (May Arts); decorative tape (7gypsies); dye ink; railroad ledger paper; map; pen

Hoops & Bun — Genevieve Simmonds
Supplies: Patterned paper (7gypsies, K&Co.); paper mesh (Magic Mesh); chipboard letters, photo corner (Heidi Swapp)

My Signature — Kristina Contes
Supplies: Cardstock; patterned paper (7gypsies, Hambly, KI Memories, Knock Knock, Making Memories, SEI, subway map); chipboard letters (Heidi Swapp); stamps (FontWerks, Purple Onion); rub-on letters (Autumn Leaves); photo turns (7gypsies); brads; corner rounder; pen

Uniform — Erica Hernandez
Supplies: Patterned paper (Bo-Bunny, Melissa Frances, Polar Bear Press, Sandylion, Scenic Route); patterned transparency (K&Co.); chipboard letters (Li'l Davis, Scenic Route); acrylic paint; sticker accent (7gypsies); rub-on accent (BasicGrey); pen; AL Highlight font (Internet download)

Page 94: Inspiration Everywhere

Growth — Kristina Contes
Supplies: Corrugated cardboard; patterned paper (7gypsies, Chatterbox, Hambly, Scenic Route, SEI, Waste Not); patterned transparency (Hambly, My Mind's Eye); sticker accents (7gypsies, American Crafts, Avery, Doodlebug, EK Success, Heidi Swapp, Making Memories, Paper Source); rub-on accents (Hambly); stamps (FontWerks, PSX, Purple Onion); ribbon (American Crafts, May Arts, Michaels, Scrapworks); book rings; pen

You Shine On Me — Meghan Heath Dymock
Lyrics by: Dave Matthews Band
Supplies: Cardstock; patterned paper (unknown); chipboard heart and letters, decorative tape, foam stamps, paint (Heidi Swapp); chipboard bookplate (unknown); rhinestones; pen

Choo Choo Ben — Nisa Fiin
Supplies: Patterned paper (7gypsies, My Mind's Eye, SEI); plastic letters (Heidi Swapp); ribbon (May Arts); label (7gypsies); dye ink; pen

Page 98: Being a Woman

Me: Woman Mini Book — Genevieve Simmonds
Supplies: Plywood box; upholstery samples (unknown); patterned paper, stickers (7gypsies); journaling accents (Heidi Swapp); bookbinding tape (Making Memories); stamps (Lazar, Purple Onion); handmade paper scraps; charm, ribbon (unknown); staples; pen

Girl Stuff — Anja Wade
Supplies: Patterned paper (Hambly, Karen Foster); letter sticker (Me & My Big Ideas); floss; rhinestones; folder tab (unknown); corner rounder; pen

I Heart Being a Woman — Kristina Contes
Supplies: Patterned paper (7gypsies); stamp accents (Purple Onion, Teesha Moore); embossing powder; chipboard letters (Heidi Swapp); rub-on accent (BasicGrey); sticker accent (Making Memories); ribbon (Maya Road, vintage); pen

Page 100: The Little Things

Little Things — Linda Buranasakorn
Supplies: Patterned paper (BasicGrey); mini folder (Paper Source); label maker (Dymo); rub-on letters (American Crafts); chipboard heart (Heidi Swapp); epoxy letters (KI Memories); letter pins (Heidi Grace); stamp (Rubber Soul); solvent ink; metal clip (Making Memories); felt ribbon (Party Partners); thread; pen

Please Never Stop Seeing Me — Meghan Heath Dymock
Supplies: Patterned paper (Rusty Pickle); letter stickers (Heidi Swapp); rhinestones; labels (Wal-Mart); rub-on accents (7gypsies); gold accent (unknown)

I Crack You Up — Nisa Fiin
Supplies: Patterned paper (My Mind's Eye, PaperGami); labels (Paper Source); sticker accent (7gypsies); ribbon (American Crafts, May Arts); letter stamps (Purple Onion); dye ink; photo corners (Heidi Swapp); date stamp (unknown); sandpaper; pen

Always and Forever More Wish — Genevieve Simmonds
Supplies: Cardstock; chipboard; patterned paper (7gypsies, FontWerks, Urban Lily); stamps (Purple Onion); stamping ink; star accents (Heidi Swapp); gesso; staples; pen

Page 102: Tribute Page

Ma Mère — Genevieve Simmonds
Supplies: Cardstock; letter stickers (EK Success); fabric (Amy Butler); photo turn (7gypsies); thread; pen

So Handsome — Kristina Contes
Supplies: Kraft cardstock; patterned paper (magazine clippings); letter stickers (American Crafts); rub-on accents (7gypsies); pen

Gram's Ring — Jamaica Edgell
Supplies: Cardstock; patterned paper (Kate's Paperie, Paper Presentation); corner rounder; pen

Tribute: To Us — Erica Hernandez
Supplies: Cardstock; vellum; chipboard letters (Heidi Swapp); brads (American Crafts); rub-on accents (My Mind's Eye); stamp (FontWerks); dye ink; pen; map (printed from Internet)

Who Knew — Nisa Fiin
Supplies: Patterned paper (KI Memories, MOD, Scrapworks, SEI); letter and number stamps (PSX, Purple Onion); dye ink; transparent frame (Heidi Swapp); ribbon (May Arts); corner punch; brad (Making Memories); brown paper bag; paint; pen

They Make My Life Brighter — Anja Wade
Supplies: Cardstock; patterned paper (Autumn Leaves); letter stamps (Educational Insights, Wal-Mart); stamp accent (FontWerks); floss; sticker accent (EK Success); embroidered accent (Wrights); pen

Aubrie Jane — Meghan Heath Dymock
Supplies: Cardstock; patterned paper (7gypsies, Autumn Leaves, Making Memories); rhinestones (Heidi Swapp); wing accents (Autumn Leaves); sticker accents (Doodlebug, K&Co., Making Memories); labels (Li'l Davis, Making Memories); acrylic paint; flower sticker (EK Success); woven letters (Scrapworks); photo corner, ribbon (unknown); staples; pen

Page 106: Why I Scrap

I Scrap — Genevieve Simmonds
Supplies: Cardstock; patterned paper (7gypsies); patterned transparency (Hambly); chipboard letters, decorative tape (Heidi Swapp); envelope (office supply store); notebook paper; staples; pen

For the Future — Jamie Bagley
Supplies: Cardstock; patterned paper (Making Memories); letter stamps (Autumn Leaves, FontWerks); stamp accents (Heidi Swapp, Hero Arts, Plaid); solvent ink; quote bubble (Bam Pop); ribbon (unknown); pen

Gone — Jessica Fulkerson
Supplies: Cardstock; patterned paper (7gypsies, Scrapworks); rub-on letters (Autumn Leaves); tags (Making Memories); rub-on accents (BasicGrey); die-cut flowers (All My Memories); brad; SP Wonderful Wendy font (Scrapsupply)

Why I Scrapbook — Nisa Fiin
Supplies: Patterned paper, rub-on accents (Hambly); sticker accents (KI Memories); stamps (Purple Onion); dye ink; staples; pen

Freeze Time — Kristina Contes
Supplies: Vellum (Paper Source); rub-on letters, transparency (My Mind's Eye); stamps (Purple Onion); rub-on accent (Hambly); sticker accents (7gypsies, EK Success); embossing powder; pen

The Point Is To Remember —
Meghan Heath Dymock
Supplies: Cardstock; chipboard letters and stars (Heidi Swapp); acrylic paint; letter stickers (KI Memories, Making Memories); pen

Page 110: Friends

Why Can't We Be Friends — Nisa Fiin
Supplies: Patterned paper (My Mind's Eye); ribbon (May Arts); letter stickers (American Crafts); acrylic paint; metal frame (Scrapworks); file label (unknown); staples; pen

These Girls — Kristina Contes
Supplies: Cardstock; patterned paper (Paper Presentation); ribbon (M&J); word stickers (7gypsies); labels (Paper Source); letter stamps (FontWerks); embossing powder; mirror accents (unknown); staples; pen

Who Knew? — Jamie Bagley
Supplies: Patterned paper (A2Z, BasicGrey, CherryArte, Doodlebug, KI Memories, Making Memories); corkboard; letter and accent stamps (FontWerks); date stamp (Making Memories); solvent ink; decorative punch, sticker accents (EK Success); heart brad (Creative Impressions); misc. accents (magazine clippings); pen

100 Percent? Yes — Genevieve Simmonds
Supplies: Envelope; transparency; floss; letter stamps (Purple Onion); rub-on accents (FontWerks); solvent ink; staples; ribbon (unknown); pen

Page 112: Collections

Revenge of the Nerds — Linda Buranasakorn
Supplies: Patterned paper (American Crafts, BasicGrey); rub-on letters (American Crafts); typewriter; date stamp (Making Memories); stamp accents (FontWerks); solvent ink; buttons (SEI); floss

Never Enough Supplies —
Meghan Heath Dymock
Supplies: Patterned paper (American Crafts); rub-on accents (American Crafts, Autumn Leaves); sparkle letter (Wal-Mart); acrylic flower, letter sticker (KI Memories); decorative tape, rhinestones (Heidi Swapp); flower accents (Doodlebug, K&Co., Making Memories); sticker accents, word plaque (7gypsies); transparency frame (My Mind's Eye); staples; pen

Fragrance — Kristina Contes
Supplies: Velvet paper (SEI); patterned paper (Peculiar Pair, Scenic Route); chipboard letters (Heidi Swapp); patterned transparency (My Mind's Eye); tab (7gypsies); ribbon (Michaels); brads; pen; Selfish font (Internet download)

Fabulous Rock Collection —
Genevieve Simmonds
Supplies: Cardstock; metal charm (Making Memories); tag with chain (from clothing); pigment ink; solder drops; pen; Babel Sans, Bill Hicks fonts (Internet download)

Page 114: Home

Family — Kristina Contes
Supplies: Cardstock; patterned paper (Ali Edwards, Chatterbox); letter stickers (American Crafts); rub-on accents (7gypsies, Hambly); sticker accents (7gypsies); stamp (Purple Onion); brads, photo turns (Making Memories); corner rounder; pen

Heath Five — Meghan Heath Dymock
Supplies: Patterned paper, epoxy stickers, labels (Autumn Leaves); letter stickers (American Crafts, KI Memories); rub-on accents (American Crafts); playing cards; pen

All That Remains — Nisa Fiin
Supplies: Patterned paper (7gypsies, BasicGrey, Chatterbox); number stickers (Headline Sign); tab (Heidi Swapp); letter stamps (Li'l Davis); dye ink; acrylic paint; chipboard bookplate (BasicGrey); embellishments (7gypsies); letter stencil (unknown); brads; staples; pen

Home — Jessica Fulkerson
Supplies: Cardstock; patterned paper (BasicGrey, Scrapworks); title letters (Heidi Swapp); letter tags (Doodlebug); acrylic paint; masking tape; staples; SP Toby Type font (ScrapSupply)

SOURCES

The following companies manufacture products featured in this book. Please check your local retailers to find these materials, or go to a company's Web site for the latest product. In addition, we have made every attempt to properly credit the items mentioned in this book. We apologize to any company that we have listed incorrectly, and we would appreciate hearing from you.

3M
(888) 364-3577
www.3m.com

7gypsies
(877) 749-7797
www.sevengypsies.com

A2Z Essentials
(419) 663-2869
www.geta2z.com

Adobe Systems Incorporated
(800) 833-6687
www.adobe.com

Adornit/Carolee's Creations
(435) 563-1100
www.adornit.com

Ali Edwards - see Creating Keepsakes

All My Memories
(888) 933-8880
www.allmymemories.com

American Crafts
(801) 226-0747
www.americancrafts.com

Amy Butler Design
(740) 587-2841
www.amybutlerdesign.com

Amy Butler Design
www.amybutlerdesign.com

Anna Griffin, Inc.
(888) 817-8170
www.annagriffin.com

ANW Crestwood
(973) 406-5000
www.anwcrestwood.com

Around The Block
(801) 593-1946
www.aroundtheblockproducts.com

ARTchix Studio
(250) 478-5985
www.artchixstudio.com

Artgirlz
(401) 323-2997
www.artgirlz.com

Autumn Leaves
(800) 588-6707
www.autumnleaves.com

Avery Dennison Corporation
(800) 462-8379
www.avery.com

BAM POP
www.bampop.com

BasicGrey, LLC
(801) 544-1116
www.basicgrey.com

Bazzill Basics Paper
(480) 558-8557
www.bazzillbasics.com

Blockhead Paper Arts
www.blockheadstamps.com

Bo-Bunny Press
(801) 771-4010
www.bobunny.com

C-Line Products, Inc.
(800) 323-6084
www.c-lineproducts.com

Cactus Pink
(866) 798-2446
www.cactuspink.com

Canson, Inc.
(800) 628-9283
www.canson-us.com

Cardinal Brands, Inc.
(800) 282-7261
www.cardinalbrands.com

Catslife Press
(541) 902-7855
www.catslifepress.com

Cavallini Papers & Co., Inc.
(800) 226-5287
www.cavallini.com

Chatterbox, Inc.
(888) 416-6260
www.chatterboxinc.com

cherryArte
(212) 465-3495
www.cherryarte.com

Close To My Heart
(888) 655-6552
www.closetomyheart.com

Colorbök, Inc.
(800) 366-4660
www.colorbok.com

Crate Paper
(801) 798-8996
www.cratepaper.com

Creating Keepsakes
www.creatingkeepsakes.com

Creative Imaginations
(800) 942-6487
www.cigift.com

Creative Impressions Rubber Stamps, Inc.
(719) 596-4860
www.creativeimpressions.com

Dafont
www.dafont.com

Daisy D's Paper Company
(888) 601-8955
www.daisydspaper.com

Dèjá Views
(800) 243-8419
www.dejaviews.com

Deluxe Designs
(480) 497-9005
www.deluxecuts.com

Design Originals
(800) 877-7828
www.d-originals.com

Designer Digitals
www.designerdigitals.com

Designfruit
www.designfruit.com

Die Cuts With A View
(801) 224-6766
www.diecutswithaview.com

Dollar Store, Inc.
(949) 261-7488
www.wholesale.dollarstore.com

Doodlebug Design Inc.
(877) 800-9190
www.doodlebug.ws

Dymo
(800) 426-7827
www.dymo.com

Educational Insights
(800) 995-4436
www.edin.com

EK Success, Ltd.
(800) 524-1349
www.eksuccess.com

English Stamp Company, The
www.englishstamp.com

Fancy Pants Designs, LLC
(801) 779-3212
www.fancypantsdesigns.com

Federal Stamp and Seal Mfg. Co.
(800) 333-7726
www.fessco.net

FontWerks
(604) 942-3105
www.fontwerks.com

Hambly Studios
(800) 451-3999
www.hamblystudios.com

Hampton Art, LLC
(800) 229-1019
www.hamptonart.com

Hasbro
(800) 752-9755
www.hasbro.com

Heidi Grace Designs, Inc.
(866) 348-5661
www.heidigrace.com

Heidi Swapp/Advantus Corporation
(904) 482-0092
www.heidiswapp.com

Hero Arts Rubber Stamps, Inc.
(800) 822-4376
www.heroarts.com

Home Depot U.S.A., Inc.
www.homedepot.com

Ink Pad, The
(212) 463-9876
www.theinkpadnyc..com

Jo-Ann Stores
www.joann.com

JudiKins, Inc.
(310) 515-1115
www.judikins.com

Junkitz
(732) 792-1108
www.junkitz.com

K&Company, LLC
(888) 244-2083
www.kandcompany.com

Karen Foster Design, Inc.
(801) 451-9779
www.karenfosterdesign.com

Kate's Paperie
(800) 809-9880
www.katespaperie.com

KI Memories
(972) 243-5595
www.kimemories.com

Knock Knock/Who's There, Inc.
(800) 656-5662
www.knockknock.biz

Lazar StudioWERX, Inc.
(866) 478-9379
www.lazarstudiowerx.com

Leave Memories - see Blockhead Paper Arts

Letraset, Ltd.
www.letraset.com

Li'l Davis Designs
(480) 223-0080
www.lildavisdesigns.com

Lina G' Trims & Ribbons
(866) 511-8746
www.trimsandribbons.com

M&J Trimming
(800) 965-8746
www.mjtrim.com

Ma Vinci's Reliquary
www.reliquary.cyberstampers.com

Magic Mesh
(651) 345-6374
www.magicmesh.com

Magnetic Poetry, Inc.
(800) 370-7697
www.magneticpoetry.com

Making Memories
(801) 294-0430
www.makingmemories.com

Marvy Uchida/Uchida of America, Corp.
(800) 541-5877
www.uchida.com

May Arts
(800) 442-3950
www.mayarts.com

Maya Road, LLC
(877) 427-7764
www.mayaroad.com

me & my BiG ideas
(949) 583-2065
www.meandmybigideas.com

Melissa Frances/Heart & Home, Inc.
(888) 616-6166
www.melissafrances.com

Memories In The Making
www.memoriesinthemakingwholesale.com

Michaels Stores, Inc.
(800) 642-4235
www.michaels.com

Microsoft Corporation
www.microsoft.com

Misprinted Type
www.misprintedtype.com

MOD — My Own Design
(303) 641-8680
www.mod-myowndesign.com

Mustard Moon
(763) 493-5157
www.mustardmoon.com

My Mind's Eye, Inc.
(800) 665-5116
www.mymindseye.com

Office Depot, Inc.
www.officedepot.com

Old Navy
www.oldnavy.com

PaperArtsy
www.paperartsy.co.uk

PaperGami
(612) 377-4428

Paper Company, The - see ANW Crestwood

Paper Source
(888) 727-3711
www.paper-source.com

Paper Presentation
(800) 727-3701
www.paperpresentation.com

Party Partners
(206) 323-8703
www.partypartnersdesign.com

Peculiar Pair Press
www.peculiarpairpress.com

Plaid Enterprises, Inc.
(800) 842-4197
www.plaidonline.com

Polar Bear Press
(801) 451-7670
www.polarbearpress.com

Prima Marketing, Inc.
(909) 627-5532
www.primamarketinginc.com

Provo Craft
(800) 937-7686
www.provocraft.com

PSX Design, Inc.
www.sierra-enterprises.com/psxmain.html

Purple Onion Designs
www.purpleoniondesigns.com

Ranger Industries, Inc.
(800) 244-2211
www.rangerink.com

Rhonna Designs
www.rhonnadesigns.com

Ribbon Jar, The
(503) 588-7042
www.ribbonjar.com

River City Rubber Works
(877) 735-2276
www.rivercityrubberworks.com

Roger la Borde
(877) 623-7275
www.rogerlaborde.com

Rubber Baby Buggy Bumpers - no source available

Rubber Soul
(425) 882-3333
www.rubbersoul.com

Rusty Pickle
(801) 746-1045
www.rustypickle.com

Sandylion Sticker Designs
(800) 387-4215
www.sandylion.com

Sassafras Lass
(801) 269-1331
www.sassafraslass.com

Scenic Route Paper Co.
(801) 225-5754
www.scenicroutepaper.com

ScrapArtist
(734) 717-7775
www.scrapartist.com

Scrapsupply
(615) 777-3953
www.scrapsupply.com

Scrapworks, LLC/As You Wish Products, LLC
(801) 363-1010
www.scrapworks.com

SEI, Inc.
(800) 333-3279
www.shopsei.com

Stampers Anonymous
(800) 945-3980
www.stampersanonymous.com

Stampin' Up!
(800) 782-6787
www.stampinup.com

Strano Designs
(508) 454-4615
www.stranodesigns.com

Strathmore Papers (also see Mohawk Fine Papers, Inc.)
(800) 628-8816
www.strathmore.com

Swarovski
www.swarovski.com

Technique Tuesday, LLC
(503) 644-4073
www.techniquetuesday.com

Teesha Moore
www.teeshamoore.com

Two Peas in a Bucket/Kaboose Scrapbook, LLC
(888) 896-7327
www.twopeasinabucket.com

Urban Lily
www.urbanlily.com

Wal-Mart Stores, Inc.
www.walmart.com

Waste Not Paper
(800) 867-2737
www.wastenotpaper.com

Williams-Sonoma, Inc.
(877) 812-6235
www.williams-sonoma.com

Wooster and Prince Papers
(866) 407-7111
www.woosterandprince.com

Wrights Ribbon Accents
(877) 597-4448
www.wrights.com

COOLNESS

The following is a list of websites, publications, dope artists,
awesome kit clubs and suppliers that get our creative flow going.

Check it:

Art on Paper
www.artonpaper.com

Cocoa Daisy
www.cocoadaisy.com

HOW
www.howdesign.com

Ink It!, Inc.
www.inkitinc.com

Jane
www.janemag.com

Jinky Art
www.jinkyart.com

Keri Smith
www.kerismith.com

Nylon
www.nylonmag.com

Paper
www.papermag.com

Paper Creations, Inc.
www.paper-creations.com

Paper-Ya
www.paper-ya.com

Print
www.printmag.com

ReadyMade Magazine
www.readymademag.com

Sabrina Ward Harrison
www.sabrinawardharrison.com

Scrapologie
www.scrapologie.com

Story People
www.storypeople.com

Those Were the Days
www.thedays-scrapbook.com

Your Happy Place
www.yourhappyplaceonline.com

ZingBOOM
www.zingboomkits.com

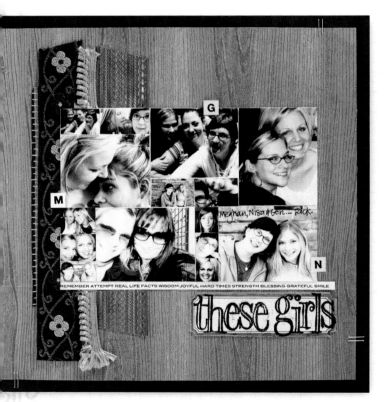

GET MORE INSPIRATION FROM THESE MEMORY MAKERS BOOKS!

IMPERFECT LIVES

Find page after page of inspiration and encouragement for capturing the "imperfect" slices of everyday life in scrapbooks.

ISBN-13: 978-1-892127-94-5
ISBN-10: 1-892127-94-6

paperback
128 pages
Z0531

TYPE CAST

Learn fresh, creative uses for a variety of type treatments as well expert tips on composing attention-getting titles and getting into the flow of journaling.

ISBN-13: 978-1-59963-003-8
ISBN-10: 1-59963-003-6

paperback
128 pages
Z0695

THAT'S LIFE

Popular scrapbook designer Nic Howard teaches you how to identify, capture and chronicle everyday moments and daily routines in your scrapbook pages.

ISBN-13: 978-1-59963-001-4
ISBN-10: 1-59963-001-X

paperback
112 pages
Z0689